THE NOTHING THAT IS

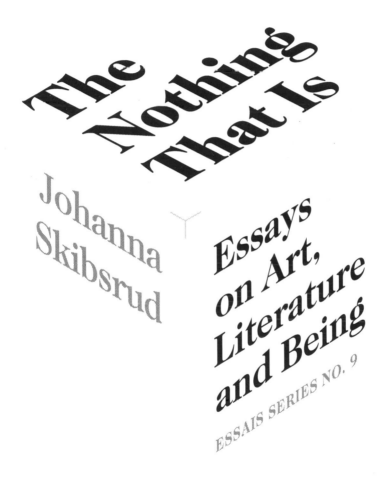

The Nothing That Is

Johanna Skibsrud

Essays on Art, Literature and Being

ESSAIS SERIES NO. 9

Book*hug Press
Toronto

Library and Archives Canada Cataloguing in Publication

Title: The nothing that is : essays on art, literature and being / Johanna Skibsrud
Other titles: Essays. Selections
Names: Skibsrud, Johanna, 1980– author.
Series: Essais (Toronto, Ont.) ; no. 9.
Description: Series statement: Essais series ; no. 9
Identifiers: Canadiana (print) 20190172975 | Canadiana (ebook) 20190173033
  ISBN 9781771665261 (softcover) | ISBN 9781771665278 (HTML)
  ISBN 9781771665285 (PDF) | ISBN 9781771665292 (Kindle)
Subjects: LCSH: Nothing (Philosophy) | LCSH: Art. | LCSH: Literature. | LCSH: Ontology.
Classification: LCC BD398 .S53 2019 | DDC 111/.5—dc23

Printed in Canada

The production of this book was made possible through the generous assistance of the Canada Council for the Arts and the Ontario Arts Council. Book*hug Press also acknowledges the support of the Government of Canada through the Canada Book Fund and the Government of Ontario through the Ontario Book Publishing Tax Credit and the Ontario Book Fund.

Canada Council
for the Arts

Conseil des Arts
du Canada

ONTARIO ARTS COUNCIL
CONSEIL DES ARTS DE L'ONTARIO
an Ontario government agency
un organisme du gouvernement de l'Ontario

Canada

ONTARIO | ONTARIO
CREATES | CRÉATIF

Book*hug Press acknowledges that we are hosted on the traditional territory of many nations, including the Mississaugas of the Credit, the Anishnabeg, the Chippewa, the Haudenosaunee and the Wendat peoples. We recognize the enduring presence of many diverse First Nations, Inuit and Métis peoples and are grateful to have the opportunity to meet and work on this territory.

IMAGE CREDITS:

p. 16: *Null Object: Gustav Metzger thinks about nothing* (Studio shot). By London Fieldworks (Bruce Gilchrist & Jo Joelson). Photo by Bruce Gilchrist (London Fieldworks), 2012. Used with permission.

p. 17: *Null Object: Gustav Metzger thinks about nothing* (Installation shot, Bluecoat Gallery). By London Fieldworks (Bruce Gilchrist & Jo Joelson). Photo by Jon Barraclough, 2014. Used with permission.

Table of Contents

For Olive and Sol

Introduction

The following essays are records of my various attempts, over the last ten years or so, to think about Nothing. I borrow my title from one of Wallace Stevens's best-known poems, "The Snowman"—a poem that through playful reflection on the tension between "something" and "nothing," presence and absence, meaning and non-meaning, distinctively demonstrates the peculiar capacity of poetic language to represent the integral, non-binary relationship between these seemingly oppositional terms.

I ask: is there a way that we can allow ourselves to dwell in paradox and contradiction and still find a way to confront what exists beyond language and form? By attending to the many different ways of thinking about and representing "nothing" in literary and artistic practice, I hope these essays will help to conceptualize this possibility, while also working to elaborate what I see as the fundamental ethical relation implicit within poetic approaches to thinking and being.

Rather than representing or describing the apparent, or what already *is*, poetry forges connections between concepts and things that would otherwise remain distinct and remote from one another—their potential and/or actual relation left invisible, unheard. These essays aim to decentre our relationship to history, as well as to a predictive or probable model of the future, by drawing attention to the way poetic language activates the multiple, as yet undesignated, possibilities replete within every moment, as well as within every encounter between a speaking "I" and what exceeds subjectivity: a listening "Other," the possibility of community, the objective world.

Despite the prevailing interpretation of poetry's etymological root, *poiesis*, as *to make*, poetic or literary language instead *unmakes* ready meaning through the playful juxtaposition of seemingly disparate subjects and objects, and by drawing attention to the inherent gap between language and the material reality that language can neither supplant nor conceal. Rather than transcending difference or producing anything, poetry points to the ultimate non-equivalence of words and things—as well as of self and world. I liken this operation to the way Luce Irigaray imagines a revitalized feminist philosophy as one that would rethink the "horizon of a reality," wherein the "other" of address would not be "overshadowed by projecting a world of one's own." According to Irigaray, the repeated error of Western philosophy is its incapacity to think past the abstract transcendental subject—a subject who, though presumably universal, tends to "see" the world from a masculine (and predominantly white European) perspective. There are obvious limitations to a philosophical design whereby, as Irigaray writes, "the whole of existing beings" are approached "from a single transcendence corresponding to the necessities of the masculine subject"—but how to move beyond these limitations is not yet clear. The essays collected here explore art, poetry, and other literatures as modes of pushing past the projection of "a world of one's own;" they argue that fundamental to a poetic approach to language and being is a space of encounter between the finite subject and what exceeds that finitude. Rather than making "something" out of "nothing," what follows is an endeavour to express the potential of language and thought to encounter what is infinitely beyond both—yet to be imagined.

"The nothing that is"

An Ethics

I. THE NOTHING THAT IS

There is nothing I can say. There is nothing I can write. There
should be a writing of non-writing. Someday it will come.
A brief writing, without grammar, a writing of words alone.
Words supported without grammar. Lost. Written, there.
And immediately left behind.

This description of a non-writing yet to come—from a late
essay by Marguerite Duras titled "Writing"—is also a
description of the poetic approach already underlying every
one of her diverse creative texts (novels, plays, essays, and films). And
yet Duras is right to cast the possibility of "non-writing" into the
future. To write, and to read, poetically is to cast beyond the perceivable limits of language and temporal being. As Michael Eskin puts
it in *Ethics and Dialogue,* poetry "unsays" ontology. It speaks not
from, or to, simple presence, but from the pre-ontological grounds
whereupon "nothing" becomes "something." In other words, poetic
writing challenges ontology by revealing and questioning the very
grounds against which we perceive, and figure, "being." It draws
attention to the very fact of those grounds—and therefore to the
interpretive process according to which ontology arises at all. At
stake in this recognition is not only the ethical question of who, or
what, can be imagined as "being," but also the questions *What are the
limits of "something" and "nothing"? What, and who, can be addressed?*

Through its emphasis on the continuous, rather than binary, relation between something and nothing, speaker and listener, Wallace Stevens's "The Snow Man" illustrates a specifically poetic possibility: that of expressing the point of contact, and therefore of potential exchange, between the representation of a finite subject or object and what refuses, or is refused, representation. The poem's negation of a coherent human subject within the figure of "The Snow Man"—described as "nothing himself"—emphasizes the capacity of poetry to test the limits of both subjectivity and discourse. It ultimately engages the reader in an unlikely encounter at the end of the poem with both "[n]othing that is not there and the nothing that is."

Although "something" is certainly suggested by both of these iterations of "nothing" in the poem's final line (especially by the use of the definite article and the copular verb in "the nothing that is"), this "something" is—in both cases—radically withheld.[1] Likewise, "nothing" in the poem can in no way be understood as a simple negation. Through a complicated "unsaying" of the grammar of subjectivity, the poem succeeds in suspending the categories of "something" and "nothing," "speaker" and "listener," "subject" and "object," "being" and "non-being," to reveal the ongoing process of interpretation that precedes—and makes possible—both experiential and linguistic access to being, meaning, and form. What the poem ultimately represents, then, is neither an abstract concept nor a perceivable "thing," but a moment of contact—immanent within every form of representation—between what is and what is not (or not *yet*) possible to perceive and understand.

"Modern poetry," Simon Critchley asserts in *Things Merely Are*, "achieves truth through emotional identification, where actor and audience fuse, becoming two-in-one." This "fusion" is usually conceived of in abstract terms, but it might equally be conceived of as a concrete space of encounter. Poetry—I argue—creates a point of potential contact and exchange by preserving the difference between the (known) parameters of the subject and/or art-object and the (unknown) other.

To think this possibility through more fully, I propose turning to *Null Object* (figure 1)—an installation created in 2012 by the UK-based London Fieldworks (Bruce Gilchrist and Jo Joelson), with the participation of artist and activist Gustav Metzger. In keeping with both the aesthetic and political goals of the "auto-destructive" art movement—for which Metzger penned the first manifesto—*Null Object* emphasizes the significance not of the object (or "non-object") produced and presented by the installation, but rather of the procedure that manifested it.

Instructed to think about "nothing," Metzger was hooked up to an EEG that measured the electrical activity in his brain. This data was then translated into a set of instructions for a robot programmed to carve out the interior of a 50-centimetre cube of 145-million-year-old Portland stone. What we confront in *Null Object* is a depiction of the point of contact between "something" and "nothing," as well as between the conceptual and the non-conceptual. The material heft and sheer size of the art object can be neither abstracted nor ignored. Even the negative space at its centre is not truly "negative," but instead the result of a set of positive instructions. Through the process of recording, interpreting, and representing Metzger's effort to think "nothing" against the material limit of Portland stone, London Fieldworks represents the way that the "null" subject is rendered legible *as* a subject in contradistinction to the "null" object it helped define.

While Stevens's "The Snow Man" asks us to recognize, and reconsider, the boundaries of something and nothing, self and other, through grammatical and rhetorical play, *Null Object* presents the point of contact and potential exchange between these categories in three-dimensional and material terms. My hope is that by reading Stevens's poem and its conceptual expression of "the nothing that is" alongside *Null Object*, we may arrive at a fuller understanding of the actual, material (rather than abstract, virtual) potential for poetry to

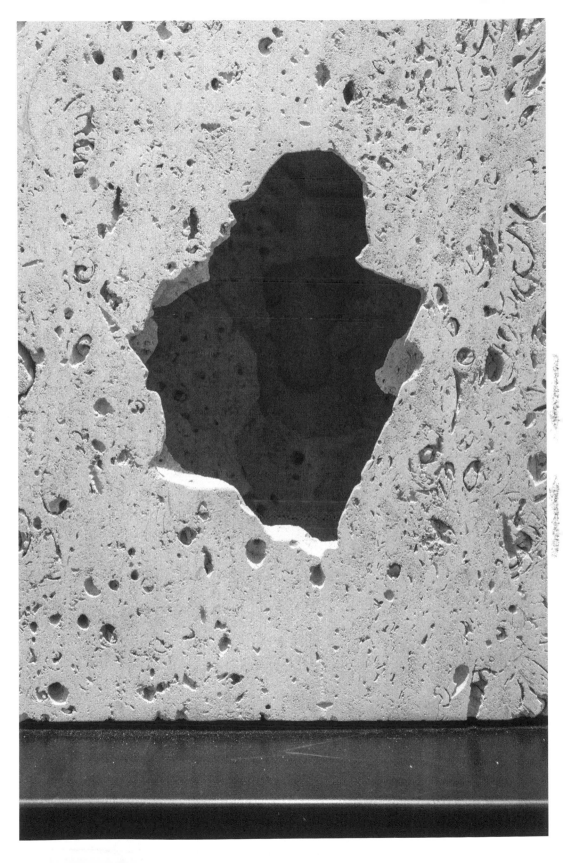

address itself beyond the borders of subjectivity and self-reflexive discourse: to become a sort of "non-writing" that is also an ethics.

I intend *ethics* here both in a broad sense—as a way of thinking the integral relationship between self and other, known and unknown—and in the narrower one suggested by Stevens in his essay "The Necessary Angel": poets should, Stevens writes in this essay, "help people live their lives."[2] To "not-write," according to Duras's use of the term, is an ethics in both of these senses. It is a resistance to the grammar of finite and self-enclosed subjectivity— and thus a resistance to the equation of self and world. It is also a commitment to locating within each word ("without supporting grammar") the point at which language touches upon, but fails to grasp, what *shapes* language by remaining utterly beyond it. To "not-write" is thus to arrive at a way of attending to what poet and theorist Fred Moten calls "difference without separability"[3]—and of locating within every perceivable power structure the real presence of what we can't, or can't *yet*, see or understand.

II. ADDRESS CIRCUITS AND CONTACT ZONES

Addressed to no one in particular, "The Snow Man" can be considered an "overheard meditation, writes Jonathan Culler in *Theory of the Lyric*. It functions like the rhetorical figure of apostrophe: an "address to the reader by means of address to something or someone else." But it also tests this formula's distinction between the apostrophic voice and the listening other by representing the essential entanglement of subject, object, and reader. By the poem's end, all three have collided within the single figure of the listener, allowing the poem to playfully disrupt a rhetorical or speech-based model of subjectivity, as well as the categories of self and other, "something" and "nothing."

The impersonal pronoun in the poem's opening line—"One must have a mind of winter"—suggests a certain procedural distance and signals objectivity and uniformity, which the rest of the poem both builds upon and undercuts. The reader participates in this depersonalizing process as it progresses via the subtraction of human faculties: intellect, sight, feeling, and hearing. By the final stanza, it is not only the subject—and object—of the poem ("the snow man"), but also the reader who can be understood to exist as "nothing himself," within the evacuated figure of "the listener."

From this position, the reader (like "the snow man") may indeed look upon, listen to, read, and know "nothing"—and thus, this "nothing" can hardly be understood as a conceptual void. Instead, the tensions and layerings between different linguistic and ontological expressions of "nothing" in the poem direct us toward a confrontation with the limits of perception and representation, inviting us to conceive of being not as a positive substance but as an interactive and an interpretive process. The poem, in other words, asks us to attend to the limits of being, knowledge, and discourse, not as lack or negation (despite its characterization of a world seemingly denuded of life and movement), but rather as an enfolding of plenitude and possibility. The snow man, the landscape, the listener—even "nothing" itself—are both there and not there. The poem itself functions as a site of indefinite, recursive, and infinitely renewable potential and exchange between being and non-being, "something" and "nothing." It allows for the possibility of contact with, rather than abstraction from, that which the subject and reader of the poem cannot yet apprehend—either because "something" has been taken for granted, or because it has been actively negated or denied.

What is described in the final line, then, within "the nothing that is," is ultimately neither ontological nor linguistic. It instead refers to a pre-ontological, prelinguistic terrain where these categories have not yet been applied or cannot yet be distinguished—not because "nothing" doesn't exist, but because the very real presence of whatever "nothing" names has so far remained invisible or has yet to be acknowledged.

By emphasizing the inherent paradoxes of referencing and representing what is ultimately unrepresentable, Stevens resists merely rebranding "nothing" as "something" (or vice versa). Instead, his poetic-ontological investigation foregrounds the continuities between subject and object, presence and absence, the finite and the infinite. Poetry, Stevens reminds us, offers a way of rethinking—and unsaying—the borders of the abstract transcendental subject by uncovering the grounds upon which those borders have been erected. It exposes us to the following questions: *What is remaindered in the process of arriving at "something"—or someone? What do language and subjectivity cover over? What are the ethical implications of perceiving and reflecting on the "something" of "nothing"?*

In his essay "Blackness and Nothingness," Fred Moten, echoing Stevens, restates the fundamental question at the root of every rigorous poetical or ethical investigation of being and language: "The question is," he avers, "Where would one go and how would one go about studying nothing's real presence, the thingly presence, the facticity, of the nothing that is?" Moten's answer—and Steven's, too—is to study the "thingly presence" of the poem.

III. "POESIS, POESIS"

Although poetry maintains a unique relationship to what exceeds the bounds of its own discourse, it is important to emphasize the continuities between poetry and other modes of knowledge production. Rather than making an exception of poetry—rarefying and ultimately isolating it from the world with which it seeks to engage—we should recognize, along with Galvano Della Volpe, that poetry, too, is a "rational and intellectual procedure" not fundamentally different from the discourses of "history and science in general." "The poet, to be a poet," writes Della Volpe in *Critique of Taste*, "has to think and reason in the literal sense of the terms. He must come to grips with the truth and reality of things...no less than the historian or the scientist in general."[4]

And yet Della Volpe overlooks an important difference between a poetic approach to "truth" and those of other rational and intellectual procedures. For poetry, the "truth and reality of things" is not something that already exists and with which the poet and the reader must "come to grips"; instead, truth is made available to poetry only through a process of interpretation wherein poet, speaker, and reader become intimately involved in the pursuit of what exists beyond all three.

"*Poesis, poesis*," writes Stevens in "Large Red Man Reading" (1950), "the literal characters, the vatic lines." Understood according to its Greek origins as *poiesis*, poetry deliberately blurs the boundaries between what "is" and what is "not yet"—what is merely possible, or yet to be imagined.[5] *Poiesis* is the process, as Giorgio Agamben puts it in *The Man Without Content*, by which something "passe[s] from nonbeing into being, thus opening a space of truth." Poetic truth is processual: it is not an abstract order of knowledge, disconnected from the speaker, listener, or the world from which it originates and to which it refers, but is instead deeply connected to the facts of both experience and language. For Stevens, as Critchley writes, "true poetry...is a poetry of fact, of fact created in a fiction," and "the truth that we experience when the poet's fictive imaginings are in agreement with reality is a truth of fact. But it is an enlarged world of fact: things as they are, but beyond us."[6]

Stevens's "The Snow Man" can be understood as a concerted attempt at articulating what Critchley calls this "enlarged world of fact," opening within "the literal characters" of representation the vatic possibility of encounter with what escapes, refuses, or is denied representation. This "vatic stance" is not at all uncommon to poetry; in fact, the lyric tradition can even be characterized by what Jonathan Culler calls its "embarrassing" habit of "invoking all manner of things, and thus presuming the potential responsiveness of the universe." Like other invocatory discourses, such as oath and prayer, poetry—as Aristotle writes in *Poetics*—is "*non-apophantic*," meaning a way of speaking that cannot be understood definitively as either "true" or "false." "The nothing that is" expresses the *non-apophantic* structure not just of poetry but of all language; the phrase thus makes perceptible the *non-actual* as grounds for the emergence of both subject and meaning. In other words: Stevens's fictive encounter with nothingness at the end of "The Snow Man" creates a *factual* basis for new articulations of the subject.

IV. NULL OBJECT

The lyric model involves a subject's address to the thingly quality of what exceeds it. This mode of address is its ethics. By speaking past the bounds of both the subject and the poem, lyric emphasizes not only the limits of subjectivity but also the possibility of crossing them. Culler refers to lyric address as "triangulated," implying fixed and singular identities for speaker, reader, and object of address— and a relatively straightforward connective path between them. The configuration of these entities in lyric poetry is rarely that simple, however, as each "point of view" often serves to undermine or "unsay," rather than definitely assert, its position. To illustrate this complexity, I propose turning to the London Fieldworks installation *Null Object*, which illustrates a variation on the lyric model and its ethical stakes. *Null Object* is a project that—like the formulation "the nothing that is"—resists easy categorization as either "something" or "nothing," formal or conceptual. This resistance to categorization foils any attempt to assign identity to what is ultimately represented, thus ensuring that the process of exchange between speaking and listening, self and other, remains radically open.

Like Stevens's "The Snow Man," "[t]he core goal of the Null Object," according to Christopher W. Tyler, "is to conceptualize the inconceivable—what it means to think about the absence of any object, the lack of an object, the non-existence of an object, and so on." But even as Tyler discusses *Null Object* in terms of absence and lack, what he describes is in fact a point of confluence and exchange between the "something" of a conceptualizing being and the "nothing" it seeks to encounter and represent. We can clearly see that in *Null Object*, for example, the negative space representing the subject forms both a gap and an opening—and can be understood to be both created *of,* and created *by,* its material conditions. That is, even though the negative shape at the core of *Null Object* presents an absence, the process of rendering that absence marks the specifically local and material nature of the subject it describes. The art object is not, in other words, an absent-minded record of abstract thought but instead a meticulous attempt at exposing the grounds that give rise to the possibility of a figure.

"Being a figure means that the contours that surround the figure are not shared but are owned by the figure alone," writes Tyler of *Null Object.* However, when we attend to what exceeds these contours by referring to it as "negative space," what would otherwise be perceived as the borderless, potentially continuous "ground" running behind the figure becomes figural to a certain extent, and the previously autonomous figure loses exclusive ownership of its borders in order to become "the continuous ground behind the negative space." Rather than a traditional figure-ground relationship, where the borders of the subject are perceived as belonging to the figure alone, poetry presents, and allows us to explore, the porousness of borders and the continuity of the spaces they delimit—wherein a figure is inextricably entangled with the grounds against which it may be perceived, and interpreted, as a speaking or listening subject.

Like the voice of the speaker in a poem (most overtly articulated by the traditional lyric "I"), the subject in *Null Object* literally "hollows out" its material conditions—but it does so without cancelling or abstracting itself. What is thus represented is not any "thing" in itself, but a negative space of confluence and potential engagement between the abstracted or unrecognized subject and the (almost literal) concrete. This tentative representation affords both an awareness and a potential unsettling of the lines according to which the "abstract" subject has been drawn. Who, or what, *Null Object* prompts us to ask, is being hollowed out by whom?

Null Object helps us to conceptualize the "inconceivable" relationship implicit within poetry between "something" and "nothing," as well as the way in which subjectivity *actually touches upon* its material conditions. Metzger's thoughts "about nothing" articulate themselves only via their contact with "something"—in this case, a 50-centimetre cube of Portland stone. Likewise, a poem like Stevens's "The Snow Man" represents what is absolutely unrepresentable by exposing the limits of language and cognition. In addressing these limits, Stevens presents "nothing" not in positive terms *as* "something," but as a positive possibility of encountering—and dwelling within—the difference between figure and ground and what exceeds, or precedes, both.

Even while evoking an imagined unity between thinking and material being, as well as between space and time, *Null Object* reminds us that there is a limit to the subject. That limit is precisely the poem's object. By formally addressing itself to the infinite without the infinite receding into a definitionless void, poetry establishes a conceptual interface between the two terms. It creates the possibility of encounter with the unknown and the other by demonstrating this interface as essential to, and indeed constitutive of, individual human being. ^

Culler writes that lyric poetry's "apostrophic wish"—"that the things of the earth function as *thous* when addressed"—renders these things, in the process of transformation, "at least in part invisible, conceptual rather than material." It is, perhaps, not difficult to understand why the apostrophic wish is often misunderstood as evasive, a space of infinite regress rather than of address and encounter. As Culler notes, even despite its establishment on the grounds of potential contact "between self and other," lyric poetry "can also on occasion be read as an act of radical interiorization and solipsism, which either parcels out the self to fill the world or internalizes what might have been thought external." But because poetic address is ultimately directed beyond the limits of the framing subject, it often results instead, as Culler argues, in "a surprisingly strong sense of prophetic revelation." ("Someday," wrote Marguerite Duras, "it will come.").

It is, in other words, precisely poetry's "embarrassing" vatic aspect—its orientation toward the radical otherness of the unknown—that grants it the possibility of escaping the interiorization and solipsism of discourses that depend upon a logic of exclusive identity, binary opposition, and narrative progression. Not only does poetry distinguish itself through its capacity to confront its own discursive borders, it also engages distinct ethical and imaginative possibilities through what Charles Altieri has called, in *Wallace Stevens and the Demands of Modernity*, "aspectual thinking." Rather than being prescriptive or ontological, poetry is speculative and prophetic—its discourse dictated not by what "is" or even what "seems,"[7] but by what should, could, or still may be.[8] The apparently impersonal and descriptive tone Stevens employs in "The Snow Man," for example, is purposely evasive—an abnegation of a more personal voice, or a fixed subjective identity. But this evasion directs us toward a new interpretive relationship between speaker and listener, self and other, and, therefore, toward a new "truth and reality of things."

Enacting the paradoxical stance of poetry—indeed, of language itself—the final affirmative negation of Stevens's poem ("the nothing that is") articulates what Christopher Tyler calls "the mind-bending confrontation between nothing and infinity." This confrontation has formed the basis of our reality at least from the time of Anaximander[9] all the way to our contemporary moment, where quantum theories posit that it is, as Tyler writes, "the infinite value of the energy at every point in empty space" from which all objects derive their finite structure.

London Fieldworks explains in their introduction to *Null Object* that the subtractive process through which a void space is created connects the concept of a limit or threshold of thought to the limit of material form. The "evanescent" quality of the work can thus be understood as a fading "into the unthought, not as something external to thought but something at the very heart of thinking." "The nothing that is" functions similarly by describing what cannot be described—the infinite, the other, the unknown—as "the very heart of" both language and being. In this way, the phrase expresses the ethics fundamental to poetry as the abnegation and, at the same time, the implicit revealing of subjective and linguistic limits. The subject both exists and does not: "there is nothing I can say. There is nothing I can write." And the poem itself is already a kind of "non-writing"— rendering language and subjectivity vulnerable to both the possibility of becoming otherwise, and of never having been.

Barbarians Among Us

The Silent Strange Poetry of a Century at War

This essay was originally delivered as part of a lecture series hosted by the Holocaust History Center in Tucson, Arizona, in fall 2014—a year that also marked the centennial of the beginning of World War I, "the war to end all wars."

Experience, after World War I, writes Walter Benjamin in his 1933 essay "Experience and Poverty," fell in value:

> Wasn't it noticed at the time how many people returned from the front in silence? Not richer but poorer in communicable experience? And what poured out from the flood of war books ten years later was anything but the experience that passes from mouth to ear.

After World War II, Paul Celan wrote, "Should, Should a man come into the world, today…he could only babble and babble…"

Theodore Adorno claimed that to write poetry after Auschwitz was itself barbaric,[1] simply a redeployment of the same language and culture that *produced* Auschwitz. He was not arguing for silence, ultimately, or for non-intelligibility, but for an acknowledgement that language and cultural production of all sorts are not only dependent upon, but *are*, in fact, the very mechanisms according to which we create our histories. Our most enlightened and most barbaric achievements and impulses are not fundamentally separated from one another, he suggests, but inherently linked.

Later, in *Negative Dialectics*, Adorno would emend his earlier statement: "It may have been wrong," he admits, "to say that after Auschwitz you could no longer write poems." A more appropriate question, he continues, is "whether after Auschwitz you can go on living." Indeed, it is not poetry alone that must be considered barbaric after Auschwitz, Adorno reminds us, but our entire culture. To choose to live within that culture, to continue to propagate it through poetry or any other established form, is to accept the basic framework of a world in which Auschwitz will continue to reoccur.

These ideas could be said to characterize the poetry of the last century. As Paul Celan suggests in "Tübingen, January," quoted above—a poem that directly references the Romantic poet Friedrich Hölderlin's spiral into madness and despair at the end of his life—if we can today only babble, it is because the world itself is mad. If there was ever an easy equation between form and meaning, or any sure route to its discovery, the poetry written in the wake of the First, and then the Second World War, assures us there no longer is. Although this leaves us without the traditional narrative moorings—a sense of logical progression, or the fixed authority of a single, reliable speaker—it also allows us to reimagine the boundaries between the past and the present, as well as between those who speak and those who are silenced.

Similarly, Adorno's indictment offers both a strategy and a possibility for poetry. While acknowledging, first, that he intended the word *barbaric* in its idiomatic or pejorative sense, *barbaric* also registers in an etymological sense. To write poetry after Auschwitz, Adorno's words suggest, is both (from the Greek) "foreign, strange, ignorant," as well (from the Sanskrit) "stammering."

Through poetry we recognize ourselves as strangers—effecting the sort of "positive barbarism" cited by Benjamin in "Experience and Poverty." Silence, Benjamin argues in this essay, affords us the opportunity to construct language anew, and in such a way as to be continuously generative rather than derivative. Operating "like any good car, whose every part, even the bodywork, obeys the need above all of the engine," innovative art and ideas adhere to "laws of their interior," Benjamin writes—but they are far from "inward." The distinction, for Benjamin, is that where "interiority" can be understood as natural and productive, affording an object or idea the possibility of propelling itself *beyond* the limits of its own structure, "inwardness" connotes internal limitation and eventual breakdown. "Positive barbarism" works deliberately against reifying "inwardness." It creates *through* language the potential to *remake* language—refusing the lineage of cultural barbarism and, thereby, "reinvent(ing) the social and political world."

To illustrate this poetic possibility, Benjamin invents a word of his own: *barbarentum*, signifying "a barbarian project" that breaks with the genealogy of the more familiar form of the word, *barbarei*. In the English translation of "Experience and Poverty," both terms appear simply as "barbarism." However, according to Maria Boletsi, in *Barbarism and Its Discontents*, although the English word *barbarism* is accurate enough for *barbarei*, a closer translation of Benjamin's unusual term *barbarentum* would be "something like 'barbarianness' or 'barbarianhood.'" Approached in this way, we see that Benjamin's *barbarentum* implicitly posits and requires a subject. *Barbarism*, by contrast—abstracted by its suffix from its active state—indicates not an active process of interpretation or a subjective identity, but instead a static condition or doctrine.

To write or to read poetry today, after Auschwitz, offers us the possibility of breaking with the genealogy of cultural barbarism by enacting the inherent *barbarianness* of language. Just as Boletsi refers to *barberei* in Benjamin's work as the "old" or "negative" barbarism and contrasts it with the "positive barbarism" implicit in *barbarentum*, perhaps we could distinguish between an "old" or pejorative *poetryism*— the sort Adorno critiques for its redeployment of the same language and set of cultural conventions that gave rise to Auschwitz—in contrast to a more active *poetryness*. The distinction could signal the idea that any transformation, as Boletsi writes, "starts with a radical renovation of language." It could also broaden our notion of what counts as "poetic"—and announce poetry as a transformative agent of change in the world, rather than as a rhetorical mode that defines or describes it.

Indeed, an emphasis on poetry's potential to effect social and political change is common to the poetics of the last century—as is a preoccupation with silence. We can trace these twinned concerns from Celan's continuous and direct evocations of silence and nothingness[2] to the incorporation of blank space in the work of contemporary Chamorro poet Craig Santos Perez, as a way of visually marking the gaps and silencing implicit within the historical record; from Allen Ginsberg's interruptive "Howl" to Terrence Hayes's confrontation with cultural silence and willed ignorance when it comes to violence against black bodies, manifested in his direct address "to my past and future assassin"; from Muriel Rukeyser's conscious attempt at providing a space for marginalized or silenced voices through her groundbreaking book of documentary poetry, *The Book of the Dead*, to M. Nourbese Philip's equally groundbreaking *Zong!*, which, by articulating the silence thrust upon murdered slaves, finds a way "to not tell the story that must be told."

All of these poets, working in the wake of the barbarisms of the past few centuries, have used their poetry to formulate and thus draw attention to different forms of silence. Their poetry is at once a call for a return to communicable experience—the sort that might pass, again, "from mouth to ear"—and an acknowledgement that there can be no return. Their words enact a barbarousness upon the language and culture of barbarism and find ways of making silence a stranger to itself.

"If I were human"

Reflections on One Hundred Years of War

Drawing from an earlier work that reflected specifically on the 2002 release of what became known as "the torture memos," this essay was revised in 2014 to mark the centennial of the beginning of "the war to end all wars."

A s Arthur Miller's 1947 play *All My Sons* opens, World War II has just ended and Joe Keller has been acquitted of the crime of knowingly shipping faulty airplane parts to American pilots overseas. Joe's younger son, Chris, has returned safely from the war, but his elder son, Larry (a pilot), has not. Joe's business partner, Steve, has been blamed and is now serving time for Joe's crime. With the exception of Keller's wife, Kate, and Steve's son, George, the characters are attempting to leave the past quietly behind.

It is a largely unsuccessful attempt. In the third act, Chris realizes he can no longer sustain the illusion of his father's innocence—and, therefore, his own. "I could jail him! I could jail him," he shouts, referring to his father, "if I were human anymore."

For Joe, to be human is to be "only human." It is to be powerless relative to the flow of events that is at once personal and historical. It is to be not-sovereign, not in control. For Chris, on the other hand, to be human is to possess the ability to transcend the parameters of one's own life in order to move toward a concept or ideal specifically outside of and beyond the self.

"No one is so foolish," wrote Herodotus, "as to prefer war to peace, in which, instead of sons burying their fathers, fathers bury their sons."

This year, we mark the centennial of the beginning of what is commonly considered the first modern war—a war that we have, perhaps, never stopped fighting. With the signing of the armistice

on November 11, 1918, the world was reimagined on entirely different lines—politically, culturally, and historically. Geopolitical
boundaries were redrawn, new countries and identities established.
We are still feeling the reverberations. In recognition of the revolution in warfare technology that set World War I apart from any that
had come before, international organizations sought, for the first
time, to develop and enforce universal standards of what it meant to
be human, and what it meant to wage war. One of the earliest uses
of the phrase *crimes against humanity*, for example, was in an Allied
statement made on May 24, 1915, in response to the Armenian genocide. The statement warned members of the Ottoman government
of their *personal responsibility* for crimes that, at another period in
history, might have been accepted as the inevitable consequences of
war. But disagreements about how exactly to define and uphold the
laws of humanity would ultimately prevent the Allies from holding
Turkey accountable for its war crimes. In 1923, the Treaty of Sèvres,
which had specifically required the formation of a special international tribunal to define and assess wartime crimes against humanity,
was replaced with a new treaty that deliberately avoided any men-
tion of war crimes or genocide. This event, writes Jackson Nyamuya
Maogoto in *Reading the Shadows of History*, marked "an ignomini-
ous triumph of impunity over international justice"—and
highlighted the difficulties of legally defining and defending
"human being."

When the Swedish founder of modern taxonomy, Carolus Linnaeus,
developed the classification *Homo sapiens* (which he first identified
simply as *Homo*), he did not record, as he did for other species, any
specific identifying characteristics. Instead, he established the
human being only by, as Giorgio Agemben notes in *The Open: Man
and Animal,* "the old philosophical adage: *nosce te ipsum* {know your-
self}." Even when, later, the further designation *sapiens* was added,

the complete term could never be considered a categorical *descrip-tion*. "It is worth reflecting," writes Agamben, that this "taxonomic anomaly…assigns not a given, but rather an imperative as a specific difference." In other words: according to Linnaeus, the human being has no specific identifying characteristics that might separate him from other animals other than his ability to recognize himself.[1]

This apparently open, self-determining space of identification masks a history of violence and exclusion. We know that the borders of the human have long been vigilantly policed, and that self-determination has been granted only to a select few. In 1961, at the height of the Algerian Revolution, Franz Fanon wrote in *The Wretched of the Earth* that the "Manichaeism" of the colonial world reaches its logical conclusion in the dehumanization of the colonized subject. "In plain talk," writes Fanon, "he is reduced to the state of an animal." Sylvia Wynter has similarly argued, in "Unsettling the Coloniality of Being/Power/Truth/Freedom," that the "systemic stigmatization, social inferiorization, and dynamically produced material deprivation" of Native and Black "Others" serves to "'verify' the overrepresentation of [Western] Man as if it were *the human*, and to legitimate the subordination of the world and well-being of the latter to those of the former." In response to these urgent and necessary critiques, what we need is not new, or more particular, ways of *defining* what it means to be human, but new appreciations of the complex entanglements of *every* definition with what it excludes. We need new modes of self-reflexivity that—rather than fortifying the borders of "the human"—draw attention to the involved histories and underlying connectivities every border ultimately represents.

If we can recoup the poetic possibility buried within the philosophical adage "know thyself," we may also begin to appreciate that what it means to be human has never truly been defined. We may see that the experience of reflection and inquiry suggested by the adage is, and must be, ongoing. And that it includes us. Finally, we may see that, at our best, we are defined by our resistance to definition—by the very act of inquiry into the nature of what and who we are, and why it should matter.

Both literature and war are propelled by these unanswerable questions. Both grapple with established truths, seeking to unsettle, or re-employ, them. Both result not in definitive answers, but the re-establishment of the same age-old questions. With both we are presented—as we are in *All My Sons*—with a dialogue between pragmatism and idealism, between Joe's idea of being "human" as "what the little man does" and Chris's loftier vision of what it might mean to sublimate private concerns in service of more universal ones.

When Chris finally works up the courage to accuse his father, Joe pleads with his son to "see it human": "Chris…Chris," he says, "I did it for you, it was a chance I took for you." Chris is unwilling to accept such a seemingly small and personal explanation for his father's crime. "What the hell do you mean, you did it for me?" he asks. "Don't you have a country? Don't you live in the world?" But his attack is not just directed toward Joe; he knows he has also been complicit in his father's crime. Though he did not have any direct involvement in the crime itself, he finds himself—in the face of something he knows is wrong—utterly powerless, unable to seek justice or even to understand what, in this particular context, that word might mean.

"The most hateful grief of all human griefs is this," laments Herodotus: "to have knowledge of the truth but no power over the event."

In direct contrast to war, literature offers a space of reflection within which we might consider the inherent incompatibility of truth and power, as well as the essential ambiguity at the heart of what it means to be human. As Muriel Rukeyser has written in *The Life of Poetry*, literature allows us to "encounter ourselves"—and to become, in the process of doing so, "more human." If to be human is to recognize oneself, it follows that to be "more human" is to recognize oneself more completely. Literature reminds us of the importance of this task—despite or rather because of the ambiguities and entanglements inherent in every attempt at definition.

Where the practice of war disrupts boundaries only in order to establish new ones, the practice of literature involves both implicit and explicit acknowledgement of the partialities and complexities involved in every narratable event and point of view. Literature allows us to recognize our agency both as interpreters of history and as actors within our contemporary moment by figuring the relation between cause and effect, the past and the future, self and other—and by encouraging a range of emotional response to the consideration of those relations. In *Wired for War: The Robotics Revolution and Conflict in the 21st Century* [SRI], Peter Singer tells us that it is literature, more than any other discipline, that has proved most prescient in prefiguring scientific and technological advancements, including the development of war technology, because its imaginative capacity remains unrestricted by "the constraints of a budget or lab, time or bureaucratic politics." Literary works such as H.G. Wells's *War of the Worlds* (which inspired the scientific advancements that led to the moon landing), George Orwell's *1984* (which predicted our contemporary surveillance culture), and Isaac Asimov's short story, "Runaround" (which continues to influence ethical thinking around artificial intelligence) show that literature is often able to both anticipate the direction of scientific and technological advancement and foresee the sort of sacrifices certain technological advancements might entail.

Today, as Singer writes, it's still the hope of many analysts that the use of unmanned weaponry in warfare will usher in "a very different age," perhaps even "a more human one," but modern developments in war technology also introduce a whole new element of unpredictability onto the battlefield. Although robots may succeed in reducing some of the "fog of war" with their hyper-focus and quick reflexes, what's missing—at least at this point in their development— is an emotional intelligence that would allow them to process the nuances of complex situations, and then to react appropriately. Also, though unmanned systems may reduce the number of servicemen employed in the field, they significantly "lower the threshold for going to war," writes Singer. He is blunt on this point:

> Unmanned systems represent the ultimate break between the public and its military. With no draft, no need for congressional approval (the last formal declaration of war was in 1941), no tax or war bonds, and now the knowledge that the Americans at risk are mainly just American machines, the already lowering bars to war may well hit the ground.

Whereas war used to imply real physical displacement and risk, it is increasingly becoming a virtual reality. This gap between cause and effect, apparent and real, will only continue to widen as militaries employ more unmanned systems and as those systems become more autonomous. Additionally, because of how quickly technological innovations are being made, and how "unreal" many of them still seem to governments and policy-makers, there is a prevailing "legal limbo" when it comes to robotics in warfare. Singer notes, for example, that no prohibitions have yet been made against robots making life-or-death decisions. This is dangerously problematic since, as many analysts see it, machines still lack the "human element"—that is, the capacity for self-reflexivity and empathetic response. As the robotics industry advances in other fields, especially as companions for humans (only the sex industry rivals the military complex in terms of research spending), it will be our own empathetic response *toward* machines that will increasingly blur the definition of what it means to be human—as well as what it means to wage war.

"No one is so foolish as to prefer war to peace, in which, instead of sons burying their fathers, fathers bury their sons." What appeared self-evident to Herodotus is called into question today by the changing nature of how humans (and robots) wage war. Although we will no doubt continue to be affected by—and endeavor to protect ourselves against—our own losses, the increasingly abstract, and mechanized, nature of contemporary warfare may lead to a gradual disassociation from the violent emotional rupture Herodotus describes. When we no longer retain a fundamental sense of the human impact of war and cease inquiring after, or reflecting upon, our individual and collective responsibility when it comes to embarking upon or waging it—this, I argue, is the point at which we cease to be human.

Miller's *All My Sons* is, in this sense, a thoroughly human effort. It is also, ultimately, an optimistic one. As Jeffrey Mason observes, Miller asked that his characters—as well as, implicitly, his readers— "assume responsibility for their society and act on the belief that action can lead to results; his is a clarion call to activism." Though Miller's play lays bare the limitations of action as well as the "moral ambiguities" that sometimes proceed from our actions, the imperative is nonetheless clear: *nosce te ipsum*—know yourself. For Miller, it is the individual's sense of duty or conscience that moves him beyond the scope of a sometimes disastrously limited personal vision. And yet, for his characters, there never is any clear path. Over and above a capacity to define the parameters of a moral centre, it is a capacity to acknowledge the essential ambiguities and entanglements of every moral choice that constitutes true self-recognition, and establishes a place from which to act. To be human, in other words, is to be both "only" and "more" human; it is to recognize and accept the tremendous risk—and accompanying responsibility—of remaining undefined.

"The horror, the horror"

False Atrocity Tales, Fake News, and the Problem of the Authentic Image

This essay first appeared in Brick *99 (Summer 2017).*

On the night of October 21, 1967, my father, Lance Corporal Olaf Skibsrud, twenty-one years old and serving as a marine in Vietnam, witnessed the murder of a civilian woman at the hands of one of his superiors. Deeply troubled by the incident, he reported it to the company chaplain, and an Article 32 investigation ensued, in which my father and several other witnesses were called to testify. The transcript of my father's testimony, excerpted from the five-hundred-page document produced during the investigation into the still-controversial events surrounding what became known as "the incident at Quảng Tri," was forwarded to me in 2006 by my father, who had received it from historian Gary Kulik, then at work on his own account of the event.

A decorated veteran of the Vietnam War, Kulik had served as a medic in the same company as my father and had heard rumours of the Quảng Tri affair at the time it occurred. Later, he became aware of the version of events recorded by former marine Terry Whitmore in his 1971 memoir, *Memphis–Nam–Sweden: The Story of a Black Deserter*, in which Whitmore claimed that more than three hundred civilians were killed in Operation Liberty II at Quảng Tri. Whitmore's version of the incident seemed blatantly fabricated—one of many false atrocity tales that became increasingly common toward the end of, and following, the Vietnam War. These were stories that exaggerated, or even seemed to brag about, the horrors of veterans' experiences, as if in answer to the civilian perception of an increasingly unpopular war.

Kulik concludes his 2009 account of the war, *War Stories: False Atrocity Tales, Swift Boaters, and Winter Soldiers—What Really Happened in Vietnam,* by saying:

> The reason to expose false atrocity stories is so we can retain our outrage at true atrocity stories. Otherwise it's all noise, feeding into the widespread belief that atrocities defined American conduct in Vietnam. The credulous belief in such stories dishonors the service of those soldiers who acted with honor, who did not kill Vietnamese villagers, and who were not party to covering up the killing of children.

But even as Kulik attempted to lay to rest the false atrocity stories that had emerged during and in the wake of the American conflict in Vietnam, a new generation of stories with an even murkier relationship to "truth" and "falsity" was emerging. Where atrocity tales from the Vietnam War and earlier conflicts could easily be deemed incredible due to a lack of documentation, in an era of social media, "fake news," and a steady onslaught of information and images representing every imaginable "point of view," it is documentation itself that has become incredible.

Journalists have long acknowledged the uncertain relationship between the presentation of facts and the facts themselves. Always wary of the possibility of their own implicit bias, they have avoided drawing a hard line between truth and falsity in the stories they report. But with a sharp increase in "fake history" and "fake news" leading up to and following the 2016 US general election, many journalists have begun to rethink their attitudes toward these categories and—as Charles Taylor puts it in a recent article published in the *Boston Globe*—to call "a lie a lie." In his 2017 response, *Wall Street Journal* editor-in-chief Gerard Baker defended the profession's skepticism with regard to categories of truth and lie, warning against becoming too comfortable with the word *lie*: "*Lie* implies much more than just saying something that's false," he contends in "Trump, 'Lies,' and Honest Journalism." "It implies a deliberate intent to mislead." The term, "lie," he argues further, "conveys a moral as well as factual judgment." Instead of making such judgments, journalists should present their readers "with the facts.

The desire to sort fact from fiction and truth from lies may feel especially urgent today. But at a time when "fake news" has become a political buzzword, used for contradictory purposes, and our collective history has become so heavily mediated that, even while it is happening, it often feels fake, how do we begin to reclaim these crucial distinctions? It is not for nothing that we have developed an appreciation of the dangerous and essentializing nature of truth claims—or their summary dismissal—or that we have learned to recognize the inherent partiality of every form of representation, including the ways in which even a seemingly objective medium like photography relies heavily upon, and sometimes exploits, the imagination. A critical approach to media in all of its forms and a resistance to believing everything we read, hear, or see is prudent—even necessary—today, and yet such circumspection can also obscure the very real issues that every form of media, like every human being, subjectively and partially conveys.

When Kulik dismissed Whitmore's account of Operation Liberty II because of its subjective and undocumented nature, he also dismissed the complicated relationship atrocity tales have always had with the categories of truth and falsity—including the question of why, if the story was false, Whitmore chose to account for his experience that way. When atrocity tales are obscured or dismissed today due not to a dearth but instead to an excess of documentation, we risk swinging heavily in the opposite direction and dismissing the complicated relationship that subjective, always partial documentation has to the facts.

The case of the Abu Ghraib "hooded man" photograph from 2003 is one example of this contemporary tendency to focus on the potential unreliability of subjective experience and its documentation, while overlooking the broader reality of which this unreliability is a part. The photograph circulated widely, causing a brief uproar among a public already ambivalent about US involvement in Iraq and the "enhanced interrogation techniques" that were now, apparently, being employed.

Then, in 2006, the *New York Times* published an article on the "hooded man" that featured an image of a former detainee at Abu Ghraib, Ali Shalal Qaissi, holding the infamous photograph, which he claimed depicted him. It soon came out that although Qaissi had also suffered abuse at Abu Ghraib, he was not the man in the photograph. The article was quickly retracted, and soon the established fact that Qaissi was *not* the iconic "hooded man"—that the published article was inaccurate on this point and that Qaissi had lied—eclipsed what both Qaissi and the "hooded man" photograph clearly attested to: people were being tortured at Abu Ghraib.

In his own *New York Times* article, published in 2007, "Will the *Real* Hooded Man Please Stand Up," Errol Morris investigated the "central role that photography itself played in the mistaken identification, and the way photography lends itself to those errors and may even engender them." It may be, Morris suggested, that an emphasis on documentation over a more comprehensive and intimate (and thereby more complex) approach to the people we encounter, the issues we explore, and the stories we tell can lead us toward a veracity that has very little to do, in the end, with truth.

In 2006, my father was just as skeptical about Kulik's project as Kulik was about Whitmore's. "He wants the 'facts,'" he told me after Kulik first contacted him by telephone. The irony in his voice was thick. Still, after some initial resistance, my father complied with

Kulik's request. He reported his own story dutifully, in the same spirit as he had in the initial investigation: "Well, sir, I've only answered the questions that have been asked to the best of my ability."

Forty years later, my father's account of the incident was more or less consistent not only with his original testimony of November 22, 1967, but also with the official US record of civilian deaths; because of this, his story soon became central to Kulik's historical account of the operation. That this should be so is, at the very least, worthy of some reflection. Even one month after the incident in question, my father's description of the events and his confidence in his own reliability were tentative at best. He said then—and afterwards it was even clearer to him—that he had witnessed the incident in a state of emotional shock. No doubt based on what he saw as the provisional quality of his own memory and experience, he wondered openly if the "facts" in this case had ever existed at all.

Morris writes of the "hooded man" photograph: "Believing is seeing, not the other way around." What we "see" is determined not by any accessible objective reality but by our most deeply held predispositions and expectations. An insistence on establishing the authenticity of the images and narratives presented to us often obscures our deeply ingrained prejudices, ideals, and beliefs. Facts, says Morris, are very much like photographs in that they allow us to think we know more than we really do. "With the advent of photography, images were torn free from the world, snatched from the fabric of reality, and enshrined as separate entities. They became more like dreams. It is no wonder we really don't know how to deal with them."

A US Marines spokesperson, Captain Kendra Hardesty, articulated the tentative and troubled relationship media images have with reality when, following the release of a video in January 2012 that depicted four Marines urinating on a dead man, she said, "While we have not yet verified the origin or authenticity of this video, the actions portrayed are not consistent with our core values and are not indicative of the character of the marines in our corps."

By emphasizing the possible unreliability of the documents, Hardesty managed to direct the conversation past the (present, apparent) documented reality and toward an (absent) rhetorical one. Rather than believe what we see, in other words, Hardesty asks us to put our faith in what we would *like* to see, what we would *like* to believe. She destabilizes the image by directing our attention to its essential and irremediable separation from the reality it represents. What, after all, is a truly verifiable or "authentic" image?

Morris explores this question by comparing two available versions of Roger Fenton's "Valley of the Shadow of Death" photograph taken in 1855 during the Crimean War: one depicts a stretch of road littered with cannonballs and the other depicts the same road cleared. Which photograph is original and authentic, Morris asks in *Believing Is Seeing*, and which one is posed? On second thought, "couldn't you argue that every photograph is posed because every photograph excludes something?"

What we fail to see when we confront the 2012 urination video or the hooded man photograph is that what we see really *is* what we see. These images—even if difficult, partial, "unofficial," or limited in scope and point of view—reflect the reality in which we live, a reality that fundamentally includes ongoing problems of judgment and interpretation.

"And so," Kulik concludes in *War Stories*, "a Vietnamese woman died that morning—shot in the back in front of her children. Mourn for her. She did not deserve to die in that way." The definitiveness with which this conclusion is drawn—and with which Whitmore's account of more than three hundred civilians having died that night is dismissed—is based largely on the aligning testimonies of two men: Private First Class Ronald P. Toon and my father. "Whitmore lied," Kulik resolutely declares:

He didn't exaggerate. He lied. An exaggeration is when you claim that fifty Vietnamese were killed, when ten were, or twenty. He claimed that an entire village was wiped out— 300 or so Vietnamese. He offered graphic depictions of those killings—killings that never happened.

It is worth noting that in his attempt to put to rest one of many false atrocity tales from the Vietnam War era, Kulik includes the testimony of a man who once suggested to me that if I truly wanted to understand the Vietnam War, I'd be "better off watching the movies. Brando in *Apocalypse Now*, for instance."

In suggesting that I might learn more from what is, perhaps, the paramount false atrocity tale of the Vietnam War than I ever could from him, my father never intended that the film reflected his, or indeed anyone's, direct personal experience, as I at first fleetingly supposed. (I remember I laughed out loud, thinking he was joking.) He was suggesting instead that a quality of that experience—a profound sense of confusion and of horror; a sense, indeed, of the *un*reality of the experience—was accurately conveyed in the film. What had been evidently important to my father was not the "facts" that he had spent such a long time trying to forget, but the horror, pain, guilt, and confusion that he never would. Implicit also in his suggestion is the idea that our realities are always and necessarily constructed to a certain extent by unreality—by what we can hardly perceive, let alone express or understand.

And yet, if we become too comfortable with this idea, as perhaps we already have, we risk losing our collective capacity for outrage not only at false atrocity stories but at any "deliberate intent to mislead." As Kulik has claimed regarding Whitmore's account of Operation Liberty 11, "the credulous belief" in false stories dishonours those who behave honourably and those who continue to believe in the difference between fact and fiction, truth and lies. This is an important point, but the problem of why such a vast number of false atrocity tales arose from the Vietnam War is only partially solved by asking the questions *Which ones are true?* and *Which ones are false?* We need also to ask, *What is it about contemporary wars that encourages this form of storytelling?* and *Why do the soldiers who fight them want so badly to identify not as heroes but as victims?* Similarly, if we want to reclaim the difference between "truth" and "lies" in contemporary politics and journalism, we must consider not only the question of how we might begin to call "a lie a lie" but also the question of how, and why, we have arrived at a point where so many of us are willing to believe stories that are, as Baker puts it, "as far as the available evidence tells us, untruthful."

Not only does the true-false distinction fail to address the complexities of our current media climate and, similarly, of contemporary atrocity tales so often characterized by the vagaries and limitations of documentation itself, it also fails to tell us anything about what motivates real atrocities, or anything about the horror of experiencing them.

I began corresponding with Kulik while writing my first novel, *The Sentimentalists*, a work of fiction that includes excerpts of my father's real-life testimony and that explores the uncertainty that arises whenever two very different approaches to truth and the historical record collide. I had received Kulik's contact information from my father and, in 2009, one year after my father's death and shortly before the publication of my novel, I decided to get in touch to discuss my father's transcript. At the time, Kulik was still at work on *War Stories*, and after a pleasant email exchange, he requested that I take a look at the profile he had written of my father, correcting any factual errors if I found any. There were a few, and I complied with his request. In return, I asked Kulik if he would be willing to read the Vietnam sections of my novel, again correcting any errors. My father had made me well aware of Kulik's approach to Operation Liberty II, so I was careful to emphasize that my own project was literary rather than historical, my motivation not to reveal the facts but to explore the manner in which they intersected with fiction. Kulik agreed to read the excerpts, but after I provided them, our once-cordial correspondence stopped abruptly. Kulik asked me not to contact him again, and not to ask why.

I can only imagine now that our particular senses of how and for what purpose historical events should be explored and treated were finally too dissimilar. And though I did not believe—and certainly did not *want* to believe—that my project contributed to mere noise on the subject of Operation Liberty II, "the incident at Quảng Tri," or the war in general, I was sufficiently bothered by Kulik's response that a part of me feared this was the case. Where Kulik was interested in "facts," I was interested in what I could best describe as the spaces between those facts—and that is a far less comfortable place to stand.

A year later, however, reading Kulik's *War Stories*, a very different understanding of the phrase "it's all noise" occurred to me. I suddenly thought, That's it. *Noise.* That's *exactly* the material out of which our realities are constituted. It was for this reason that my father had cited *Apocalypse Now* as the most accurate record he could think of to express his experience, though, really, nothing about that movie resembled his experience at all.

What literature, history, politics, and, most essentially, language attempt is to create form from chaos, meaning (and even sometimes music) from noise. We need to attend to—and believe in—the distinction between chaos and form, noise and meaning, but also to remember that no distinction is ever absolute or escapes the contingency of noise.

It is only when we are able to accept this fundamental connection between noise and meaning that we have any hope of moving past an impotent outrage at false stories toward a more far-sighted and thorough interrogation of what's beneath, and beyond, those stories. It is only when we are able to accept that lies are also, and inevitably, a part of the truths we either accept or refuse, that we have any hope of approaching the *true* horror of the conflicts that continue to be an integral part of our reality—whether we "see" them or not.

"Refloating" the Falling Man

Philippe Petit's High-wire Act

This essay, written shortly after the 2008 election of Barack Obama, recalls the wave of optimism felt by the American left around that time—and the trepidation over how to sustain it.

"We ascribe beauty to that which is simple," wrote Ralph Waldo Emerson in an essay in 1860, to that "which has no superfluous parts; which exactly answers its end; which stands related to all things; which is the mean of many extremes." In this essay, however, it is not "simple" beauty Emerson calls for, but rather that which *is* superfluous; that which, in shaking us from the sleep that "lingers all our lifetime about our eyes," is able to move us beyond the limits of our own imaginations. Excessive beauty effects change, Emerson writes. It is the "affirmative principle," which he defines as a "superfluity of spirit for new creation." "Ah," he laments, "that our Genius, were a little more of a genius."

Emerson uses the word *superfluity* to refer not to an unnecessary excess but to what he sees as a necessary one; it points to the "human desire to go beyond [the] usual stopping places," writes critic Richard Poirier in *Poetry and Pragmatism.* While "linguistic and cultural necessity" require that deference be paid to these stopping places, "an Emersonian tries as adroitly as possible to move away from them. His superfluousness is an effort to refloat the world, to make it less stationary and more transitional, to make descriptions of it correspondingly looser, less technical, more uncertain." It is precisely this "superfluousness," in the Emersonian sense, that makes Philippe Petit's high-wire walk of 1974—re-envisioned in the 2008 James Marsh documentary *Man on Wire*—so striking. In its desire to go "beyond the usual stopping places," Petit's act invites what is, according to Emerson, fundamental to any attempt at effecting "new creation": a radical shift in the perception of the world around us. Suspended 110 stories in the air, the figure of Philippe Petit not only offers the viewer a renewed sense of the possibility for a triumphant version of the Emersonian individualism that has always been integral to American identity, it also provides a powerful antidote—albeit anachronistically—to the painful imagery of September 11's "falling man."[1]

Ironically, back in 1974, it was precisely the extreme individualism of Petit's Twin Tower walk, as well as its resistance to personal as well as civic stopping places, that made the act appear superfluous only in the pejorative sense. At a time directly following the American War with Vietnam, when the American government had recently squandered 58,226 American and an estimated 5 million Vietnamese lives, Petit's stunt seemed just that: a senseless endangerment of human life, an absurdly impractical flaunting of the power of the individual over the authority of both Nature and the State.

What is it, then, thirty-five years later, that we now find so compelling in the act? Indeed, there has been a significant resurgence of interest in Petit's wire-walk post-9/11: an artist's rendering of the event graced the cover of the *New Yorker* on September 11, 2006; Marsh's 2008 documentary was awarded two Sundance awards and an Oscar for Best Documentary Feature in 2009; Colum McCann's novel *Let the Great World Spin*, which centres on Petit's walk, won the National Book Award, also in 2009. What is it that we now see in the event? What do we want the image of Petit's "resistance" to say to—or about—us?

In a review of the Marsh documentary published in the *New York Times*, A. O. Scott writes: "Wisely, Mr. Marsh...never alludes to Sept. 11. That would have been both distracting and redundant, since it's impossible, while watching a movie so intimate in its attention to the towers, not to be haunted by thoughts of their fate." The retrospective embrace of Petit's act indicates a collective desire to return to a version of American individualism that was powerfully shaken by the events of 9/11: Petit's body, suspended triumphant above the newly constructed Twin Towers, provides a surrogate image, and consequently a surrogate response, to the feelings of helplessness and fear evoked by September 11's "falling man." Though Petit's Twin Tower walk may now seem charged with anterior meaning, what it affords us in the present and what it afforded back in 1974 is essentially the same. Petit invites us to *look again*—both at the towers and at ourselves.

"Why? Why?" Petit asks in Marsh's documentary, mimicking the response to his 1974 walk; "[It's] a very American, finger-snapping question…The beauty of it was there was no why…Maybe I wanted to escape my time. Maybe I wanted to see the world from a different perspective."

In his 1836 essay "Nature," Emerson writes that even the "least change in our point of view" will give the world a "pictorial air" and thereby elicit "delicious awakenings of the higher powers." It is this shift in perspective that is essential, Emerson suggests, to any understanding of the world around us. "Turn the eyes upside down by looking at the landscape through your legs, and how agreeable is the picture, though you have seen it any time these twenty years!"

This radical shift in perspective is at work in the imagery of Philippe Petit's high-wire act, and also in the "falling man" photo taken by photographer Richard Drew on September 11, 2001. "By mechanical means," both images suggest "the difference between the observer and the spectacle—between man and nature," and because of this, as Emerson contends, "a low degree of the sublime is felt from the fact…that, whilst the world is a spectacle, something in [the viewer] is stable."

Although the post-9/11 cultural response to the "falling man" image has been diametrically opposed to the response to Petit's act, both produce a heightened emotional state that prompts the viewer to participate in, rather than simply regard, what they depict. We could say that both images represent a "state of emergency,"[2] understood in a dual sense as both urgent and emergent—involved in a continuous process of what Emerson calls "being and becoming."

In the case of the "falling man," it was this heightened, *participatory* response that prompted viewers to brand the image as "distasteful, exploitative and voyeuristic," ultimately leading to its suppression. Naomi Halpern, the photo editor at the Allentown, Pennsylvania, *Morning Call*, which ran the photo on September 12, 2001, admits that her immediate reaction to the image was indeed one of "horror." Michael Hirsch, the business editor, agreed. "I felt like I was punched in the stomach," he said.

Later, Halpern would champion the image and push for its circulation, believing that its historical importance outweighed concerns about sensitivity: "There are photos in history that are flash points that really kind of get at the truth," he says in Henry Singer's 2006 documentary, *9/11: The Falling Man*. "They are hard to look at, but they tell a story. In this case, it got to the humanity in a way that other photos, even [those] that might be more graphic, did not." Hirsch, too, supported the decision to run the image: "I thought about it myself. What choice would I make? [...] And I think maybe that's the personal space that we went to with some people, where they thought about what their personal choice might be."

As Halpern and Hirsch suggest, the "falling man" photograph opened a space of acute awareness and questioning as to the limits of individual freedom and choice. It brought the American public face to face with the precariousness of their own realities, of their own ultimately extinguishable point of views.

Now, as we enter into what has been imagined as a new stage of American history, it may be pertinent to consider the words of poet and activist Breyten Breytenbach, as he reflects, in his essay "Mandela's Smile," on the situation in South Africa fifteen years after the election of Nelson Mandela. How and why, Breytenbach asks, did South Africa's current reality come to differ so widely from the promise held in Mandela's election? Breytenbach explores the fundamental role of the imagination in "dreaming" into existence a kinder and more inhabitable world. "We know that 'seeing' is also an act of imagination," he writes, arguing that there are real consequences to the ways in which we are able, or unable, to imagine our world. Similarly, for Emerson, the power to change, to invent, and to reinvent the world exists precisely in the generative imaginative act. "Life only avails," he wrote, "not the having lived. Power ceases in the instant of repose; it resides in the moment of transition from a past into a new state."

This "superfluous" impulse to move beyond what "is" remains the driving force behind both American exceptionalism and American individualism. It is perhaps for this reason that the image of the falling man was so injurious. Unlike other images published widely post-9/11, *Falling Man* depicts no anguish, no protest—only what looks very much like a state of repose. Halpern says: "I saw grace, I saw a stillness, even though I knew that he was falling. I saw a quietness."

Is it this *quietness* that was, and remains, so disturbing about the photograph? Possibly. But we should remember that this "quietness" was first created through the flash of Richard Drew's camera, and then judiciously selected. When the image is viewed alongside the many others Drew shot that day—images that depict the falling man in *various* poses—it becomes clear that if we glimpse a moment of repose in the image, that "repose" is not the falling man's, but our own. We have, it turns out, simply *dreamed up* the falling man. And so—as Tom Junod argues, also in Singer's documentary film—it is up to us to confront him: "We can't hope to understand these incredible times unless we look at these images and accept the witness of these images. And I think [to look] at the falling man, and to discuss it, is the only option that we have, given that there is a falling man."

Echoing and elaborating on Junod's sentiments and also Emerson's concept of "superfluity," Breytenbach contends that we must witness the extremes and then see or imagine beyond them. He writes:

> Perhaps we know no more than those who preceded us, but it is just as true that we have to transcend our limitations, that we must cling to the notion of a utopia (call it "clean and accountable government" or "common sense") as justification and motivation to keep on moving and making noise. For the mind has to be allowed to dance, even with death.

This courtship and play with death is, perhaps, what we find so enthralling in the imagery of Philippe Petit's high-wire act—especially now, when it has renewed appeal as counter-emblem to the apparent passivity of the falling man. As Petit explains in Marsh's documentary: "wire-walking is framed by death." Watching *Man on Wire*, this backdrop is all too apparent. Although we *know*, as we regard the images, that Petit will survive the walk, we see the way his act is implicitly linked both to American involvement in Vietnam, on the one hand (i.e., by a militant desire to promote and defend American values), and to 9/11 on the other (by a militant attack against those values). Like Petit, we are suspended in the negative space between two lost objects—within a space of blankness, uncertainty, and our own ignorance of what is to come.

This unlikely position grants us the possibility of a new perspective—one that permits us, in the words of Breytenbach, to "dance, even with death." That is, Petit's performance offers us a suggestion of how we might live not in *defiance* of death, but rather *because of* and *alongside* death. To choose to live in this way is not "simple," and

it is the furthest thing from passivity or "repose." It requires a radical
shift beyond our own limited perspectives and demands new, creative
combinations of experience and the imagination.

Imagination, Breytenbach writes, "gives access to 'meaning.'" It allows
us to continuously remake ourselves. Petit's act, and our imaginative
reclamation of it post-9/11, has given new meaning to the Twin Towers,
and to the acts of the imagination those towers were. It has provided
us with the occasion to turn our "eyes upside down"—the opportunity
to create new, positive possibilities for the future by confronting the
very real absences, erasures, failures, and losses in our past.

It is impossible not to be strangely, anachronistically haunted by
the fate of the Twin Towers while watching Petit realize, above them,
a most inconceivable dream. As A. O. Scott writes:

> It is easy to imagine that, in contemplating the scale and
> solidity of those brand-new towers, Mr. Petit saw them at
> least partly as the vehicle of his own immortality (whether
> or not he survived the crossing). No one looking up at the
> New York sky on a hazy morning 34 years ago and seeing a
> man on a wire could have suspected that the reverse would
> turn out to be true.

Petit has, indeed, immortalized the Twin Towers for us in their ideal
form—not through the images that survive, but through his own
superfluous imaginative act. The image of the falling man, on the
other hand—despite Junod's call to confront, come to terms with,
and even to celebrate the image—remains relatively stigmatized and
obscured. Though it, too, goes "beyond all the usual stopping places,"
forcing us to "turn our eyes," as well as our hearts, "upside down," the
falling man image depicts, in the end, an *end*: a momentary, imagined repose, but a repose nonetheless.

By contrast, Petit's act suggests another possibility: the possibility of *not* falling, of *never having to fall.* It is in this sense that Petit's high-wire dance can be seen as the falling man "refloated"—as an image of (in Petit's own words) the "exercise of rebellion" that still exists at the imaginative root of the American dream.

It is clear that this dream has yet to be realized. Moreover, it is the very act of dreaming in lieu of any real awareness, or change, that has proved a nightmare for so many, and for so long. How, then, might we confront the limits of our imaginations without either restricting or undermining our capacity to creatively remake ourselves and our world? Revisiting Petit's high-wire walk, we find a poignant reminder of the power of individual acts of the imagination. It is incumbent upon us, now, to recognize the potential power of *collective* imaginative acts. We should also acknowledge that if the dream does not manifest itself in reality, it is not because dreaming is superfluous. Rather, the dream has not yet gone far enough.

Absence in "The System"

John Ashbery and Poetic Difference

"From the outset it was apparent that someone had played a colossal trick on something," writes John Ashbery in "The System," a long poem from his 1989 collection, *Three Poems*. The line is characteristic of Ashbery's poetics: beginning in media res, it is constellated by non-definite quantifiers ("something," "someone") without direct, or even indirect, antecedent. But this is no trick. "From the outset," Ashbery refuses conventional systems of signification and begins by both illustrating and enacting the dislocation of the poem's subject from any possibility of a fixed centre:

> The one who had wandered alone past so many happenings
> and events began to feel, backing up along the primal vein
> that led to his center, the beginning of a hiccup that would,
> if left to gather, explode the center to the extremities of life,
> the suburbs though which one makes one's way to where
> the country is.

Through verbal indirection, Ashbery opens his poem onto an almost limitless field of possible meanings—and, thus, to no specific meaning at all.

"Is it then," the poem asks next, "that our bodies combined in such a way as to show others that we really mean it to each other—is this really all we ever intended to do?" Even in posing the question, the speaker implies that the answer is *no*. The possibility of ever being so "combined" in order to really "mean it" is curtailed by the impossibility of the proposition's "meaning" anything at all. The "it" of "mean it" is in fact doubly removed from direct signification in that, already serving at the sentence level as a dummy pronoun—syntactically but not semantically required—it further fails to point to any antecedent within the structure of the poem.

As Giorgio Agamben writes, in *Language and Death*, of the Italian poet Giacomo Leopardi (analyzing a poem in which Leopard repeats the pronoun *this* six times in fifteen lines), Ashbery's seemingly interchangeable and endlessly supplementable pronouns gesture toward signification without ever arriving at definitive meaning. However, instead of producing—as Agamben writes of Leopardi's idyll—a "dismayed" or anxiety-producing sense "of the interminable, of the infinite," Ashbery's playful semantic deferral suggests movement, and hidden but nonetheless evolving potential. Even the seeming finality of the poem's closing lines suggests not a final "this" but instead an ever-widening path of connection and possibility. "The allegory is ended," the poem concludes,

> its coils absorbed into the past, and this afternoon is as wide
> as an ocean. It is the time we have now, and all our wasted
> time sinks into the sea and is swallowed up without a trace.
> The past is dust and ashes, and this incommensurably wide
> way leads to the pragmatic and kinetic future.

We have been led, it seems, finally past discourse into what Agamben calls "the taking place of language" as possibility itself—into an event that *means* not because it refers to anything known, but because it is the very promise of meaning.

In presenting this promise through the endless deferral of direct signification, Ashbery's poetics enact a kind of haunting. Akin to Derrida's "specter" from *Specters of Marx*, "The System" is charged with "the frequency of a certain visibility. But the visibility of the invisible." It lends voice and form to "what one imagines, what one thinks one sees and which one projects—on an imaginary screen where there is nothing to see."

Ashbery's poem shows us that it is not just language that is haunted. The political is also characterized by the "very anessence of a ghost," as Derrida writes. To transform that ghost into "absolutely living reality"—as Marx proposed to do through "the motor of revolution"—is to mark not only the end of the spectral but also the "end of the political as such."

Such a revolutionary political transformation is not "*described*" by Marx, argues Derrida; it is "announced, promised, called for in a performative mode." In his analysis of the preamble to the *Communist Manifesto*, Derrida writes: "by saying 'it is time,'[1] time rejoins and adjoins itself here, now, a now that happens to itself in the act and the body of this manifestation:...here precisely is the manifesto that I am or that I operate in the work, in an act, I am myself but this manifestation, at this very moment, in this book, here I am."

Derrida describes the manner in which the speaker of the manifesto actually *becomes* the manifesto, enacting the essential anessence or promissory value of language itself. In fact, he reflects,

> one could be tempted to explain [not only] the whole totalitarian inheritance of Marx's thought, but also the other totalitarianisms that were not just by chance or mechanical juxtaposition its contemporaries, as a reaction of panic-ridden fear before the ghost in general.

It was not only the capitalist states of Europe, Derrida suggests, but also Marx's followers who were afraid of what had, as yet, no antecedent. The totalitarianisms that supplanted Marx's vision arose out of fear of its spectral nature; rather than "respect(ing) the promise, the being-promise of a promise" articulated by the manifesto, they fled from its anessence into the absolutely living reality of what they already knew.

But Marx was clear. "The social revolution of the nineteenth century cannot draw its poetry from the past, but only from the future," he wrote in *The Eighteenth Brumaire of Louis Napoleon*:

> Earlier revolutions required recollections of past world history in order to dull themselves of their content. In order to arrive at its own content, the revolution of the nineteenth century must let the dead bury their dead. There the words went beyond the content; here the content goes beyond the words.

In both of Marx's formulations of revolution—those past and those present—we encounter a surplus: words going beyond content or content going beyond words. In the latter formulation, however, the surplus transgresses the bounds of language. By evoking a future that cannot be brought into being by already-extant language or thought, Marx enacts the poetic possibility at the (empty) centre of language.

Ashbery also seeks to enact this possibility when he envisions a "lyric crash in which everything will be lost and pulverized," ready to be moulded into "new combinations and shapes again, new wilder tendencies"—an event that would be "unimaginable, in a word." This unimaginable event is precisely what "The System" endeavours to perform. Ashbery's language emerges in such a way that it calls attention to its own inability to encapsulate and transmit meaning; writing in this manner, he points to the spectre at the heart of language and asks us not to turn away. "For we are rescued," he tells us, "by what we cannot imagine."

When a thing is named—as soon as it gains a referent and exists in relation to what we already know—it begins, Derrida tells us in *Specters of Marx*, to "enter its death agony." This is perhaps why Marx, in *The Eighteenth Brumaire of Louis Napoleon*, calls for the social revolution to "draw its poetry…from the future."To displace the "dust and ashes" of received discourse, a rift must be made between sign and signified, as well as between the present and the past. This rift is what Derrida refers to as "poetic difference," and it is out of "poetic difference," Marx suggests—the sudden openness torn or revealed by a deferred or exploded centre—that the "unimaginable" may be expected to arrive.

Looking back, of course, we know that the totalitarian inheritance of Marx's words (both in terms of those who supported them and those who resisted them) have long since foreclosed on their initial, poetic promise. What Marx called the *here*, the *now*, of the "social revolution of today" has long ago collapsed into the "*over there* of the political revolution of yesterday" (Derrida)—indicating that, once again, the words have exceeded their content and not the other way around. But if we look to Ashbery's "incommensurably wide way," we must also recognize that poetry, or "poetic difference," still haunts every system, still opens within every discourse a way past discourse, still leads, unimaginably, "to the pragmatic and kinetic future."

Transcribing
the Waves

Language as a Spiritual Medium in
Virginia Woolf and Anne Carson

When F. H. Myers—inventor of the word *telepathy* and founding member of the Society for Psychical Research (SPR)—died in Rome in January 1901, American psychologist William James awaited the message Myers had promised him from beyond the grave. According to the doctor who'd been treating Myers, writes John Gray in *The Immortalization Commission*, the two had made a solemn pact: whoever died first would send a message as soon as he crossed over into the unknown. Too grief-stricken to remain in the room with his dying friend, James reportedly sat outside the open door, and—pen in hand, notebook in lap—appeared ready to diligently transcribe Myers's spectral communication. When the doctor returned, however, James "was still leaning back in his chair, his hands over his face, his open notebook on his knees. The page was blank."

The purpose of the SPR, over which first Myers, then James, and later Henri Bergson presided, was to "examine paranormal phenomena in 'an unbiased and scientific way,'" writes Gray. Like Myers, whose best-known publication is a book titled *Human Personality and Its Survival of Bodily Death*, James believed that communication could continue after death, and that, eventually, the phenomenon would be scientifically explained. A series of interconnected automatic writings, produced over several decades by various mediums, served to confirm the thesis that human personality could indeed survive "bodily death."

Gray quotes Alice Johnson, a member of the SPR, who tells us that the automatic writings collected from various mediums were characterized by their fragmentary and indirect nature. "What we get is a fragmentary utterance in one script," she explains, "which seems to have no particular point or meaning, and another fragmentary utterance in the other of an equally pointless character; but when we put the two together, we see that they supplement one another, and there is apparently one idea underlying both, but only partly expressed in each." Johnson's description of automatic writing could equally characterize the "stream of consciousness" literary technique employed by Virginia Woolf and other modernist writers; indeed, the literary term takes its name from James's influential description of consciousness in *The Principles of Psychology* as "a 'river' or a 'stream.'" Consciousness, James argued, cannot be "chopped up in bits," and neither could it simply disappear. "It is nothing jointed," he avers; "it flows."

That the most notable innovation in modernist narrative takes its name from James's writings on psychology and paranormal phenomena is more than an incidental detail. The "stream of consciousness" technique—and later postmodern literary techniques that employ fragmentation and non-linear progression—are rooted in a Jamesian sense of human psychology and spirit as multi-vocal, continuous, and— ultimately—shared. The literary implementation of "stream of consciousness" signals modernist writers' commitment to pushing beyond the preconceived boundary of language and selfhood to access what exists beyond the surface of the embodied subject—and to render inspiration (from the Latin *spiritus*: *breath*) perceivable on the page.

"There looms ahead of me," Woolf once confided to her diary,

> the shadow of some kind of form which a diary might attain to. I might in the course of time learn what it is that one can make of this loose, drifting material of life; finding another

use for it than the use I put it to, so much more consciously and scrupulously, in fiction. What sort of diary would I like mine to be? Something loose knit and yet not slovenly, so elastic that it will embrace anything, solemn, slight or beautiful that comes to mind.

Woolf expresses a desire to move past the "conscious" domain of narrative fiction—a domain wherein, she suggests, even "disjointed" or "illogical" progressions are scrupulously ordered by their author—toward a more expansive form that extends not only to the subconscious but also to the *extra-conscious*—that is, to the "loose, drifting material of life" that exceeds the ordering capacities of the conscious mind. What "looms ahead" of Woolf, both in and as the potent (potential) form she envisions, is a way of accessing and expressing the material of life and experience outside of conscious apprehension.

    This orientation beyond the finite limits of the speaking subject is also an orientation toward "truth"—a term I understand here in Hélène Cixous's revelatory sense as that which, existing beneath or outside of representation, can only be accessed by moving specifically away from categories of language, and reason. "We have to lie to live," Cixous writes in *Three Steps on the Ladder of Writing*.

> But to write we must try to unlie. Something renders going in the direction of truth and dying almost synonymous. It is dangerous to go in the direction of truth. We cannot read about it, we cannot hear it, we cannot say it; all we can think is that only at the very last minute will you know what you are going to say, though we never know when that last minute will be.

Writing, as presented here by Cixous, is a double negative (to "unlie" is to negate a negation of truth) that does not produce a positive. It is the presentation not of any object or idea, but rather the possibility of its expression: a necessarily imaginative projection toward "the last minute," toward death. Although writing may in this way be understood as an orientation toward truth and death, it is—in itself—neither one. Instead, Cixous explicitly aligns writing with living: the deferral of the "last minute" suggesting a continuously generative beginning that is nonetheless founded upon the idea of the end. "To begin (writing, living) we must have death," she writes. Cixous's deferral presents us with an unknown, a remainder—and reminds us that truth/death is already immanent *within* writing/living.

Crucial to Woolf, as well as to other writers experimenting with techniques of fragmentation and multivocality over the course of the last century, is this notion that the supplemental "outside" is already immanent within and confluent with the "inside," or, to use James's terms, that an infinite number of sources and possible directions *outside of* human consciousness are fundamental to, and therefore already immanent within, consciousness's stream. When Woolf writes, toward the end of *The Waves*, for example, in Bernard's voice, "We felt enlarge itself round us the huge blackness of what is outside us, of what we are not," she situates us not within the flow of a limited human psyche, but at the border between subject and object, life and death. She continues:

> The wind, the rush of wheels because the roar of time, and we rushed—where? And who were we? We were extinguished for a moment, went out like sparks in burnt paper and the blackness roared. Past time, past history we went.

Although our speaker claims that this atemporal, disembodied experience lasted "but one second," the record of it extends the experience immeasurably beyond its embodied framework. "If I could measure things with compasses I would," reflects Bernard, "but since my only measure is a phrase, I make phrases ..." Language, Woolf suggests, is the elastic form that extends, beyond living/writing—beyond the ordering impulses of both the body and the mind—toward the infinite flow of truth and death. Language therefore has the capacity to measure and record not only the activity of individual consciousness but the point of contact that every individual consciousness maintains between itself and what exceeds it absolutely.

"But how describe the world seen without a self?" Bernard asks us finally, before continuing with this further meditation:

> There are no words. Blue, red—even they distract, even they hide with thickness instead of letting the light through. How describe or say anything articulate in words again? ...One breathes in and out substantial breath; down in the valley the train draws across the fields lop-eared with smoke.

In the end, for Bernard, there are no words. Subjectivity cannot be expressed except through and as breath, which is at once both the substance of being—what is continuously taken in, what sustains and indeed *becomes* the living body—and that which is always outside: what the body is obliged (in order to live) to continuously express. The subject can thus never be thought of as a closed or finite system, but instead must be recognized as a systemic relation between inside and outside, language and breath. It is not, then, that linguistic expression of the highly subjective experience of being alive is impossible, but that *expression* itself is, inherently, a movement beyond a subjective frame.

The Waves is Woolf's effort to express the process of expression itself. She probes the relationship between writing and dying and ends the book with a direct address to death itself:

What enemy do we now perceive advancing against us, you whom I ride now, as we stand pawing this stretch of pavement? It is death. Death is the enemy. It is death against whom I ride…I strike spurs into my horse. Against you I will fling myself, unvanquished and unyielding, O Death!

Although Woolf's closing passage—voiced again by Bernard—presents an antagonistic opposition between life and death, the final lyrical invocation—"O Death!"—suggests a point of possible reconciliation between two seemingly opposite realms.

Bernard's address to the beyond is followed by a single, italicized line: "*The waves broke on the shore.*" Like other purely descriptive passages in the text, which are similarly italicized and presented without quotation marks, this final line offers an apparently objective description of the natural world outside of the concerns of the characters; it thus serves to contextualize Bernard's subjective confrontation with death within a larger flux and flow. It is the waves—not Bernard, and not death—that have the final word in the novel. The "stream," made literal here as the flux and flow of the outside world, is shown to continue beyond—and thus to provide the framework for—both subjective experience and lyrical address.

Anne Carson's *Decreation* similarly addresses the limits of the subject, and of literary form, by enacting—and pushing against—the boundary between inside and outside. As Fiona Sampson's review of *Decreation* in the *Guardian* observes, what fascinates Carson above all "is the human, 'the ancient struggle of breath against death.'"

Carson borrows the title of her book from the twentieth-century French philosopher, mystic, and political activist Simone Weil. For Weil, in *Gravity and Grace*, "decreation" is the process by which we "undo the creature in us" in order to pass beyond the limits of individual consciousness and selfhood and move closer to God. In all thirteen discrete sections of Carson's text—a hybrid of verse, prose, libretto, and a screenplay—Carson explores the possibility of transcribing experience that extends beyond the limits of "bodily life." "My personal poetry is a failure," she writes, for example, in a poem titled "Stanzas, Sexes, Seductions." "I do not want to be a person. / I want to be unbearable." The speaker of the poem asks to be unborn, to exist before or beyond bodily form, while at the same time pushing against the limits of textual form through experimentation with different genres, line breaks, and blank space. Carson's language becomes literally "unbearable": it spills over, repeats, interrupts, or vanishes entirely from the page.

This disjunction is necessary to Carson's project, because—as for Woolf—language functions as an expression not of any particular subject or object but of the essential flux and flow between subjects and objects, materiality and immateriality, measure and the unmeasurable. One of the more arresting ways in which Carson indicates this continuity between subject/object, writing/living, and truth/death is through her evocation of Michelangelo Antonioni's cinematic procedure, *temps morts*, "whereby the camera is left running on a scene after the actors think they have finished acting it." Because actors continue, "out of inertia," to act into moments that "seem 'dead,'" every action recorded by Antonioni using this technique becomes an "error." In later films, the filmmaker would even continue to run the film after the actors had left the set, "as if for a while something might be still rustling around there in the empty doorway."

In Carson's own unfilmed screenplay based on the nine-hundred-year-old love story of Heloise and Abelard, she employs the *temps mort* technique through language, rather than through performance and filmic images. Heloise begins the exchange:

The camera is still running.
My time is up.
What shall I—?
*Abelard has let go his swing and flies out of the frame without
answering. Heloise continues to swing.*

Because Heloise notes that the moment she and her lover are partici-
pating in, though ostensibly unscripted, is still being recorded, their
exchange becomes an "error," a "supplement" to the agreed-upon text.
Realizing this, Abelard announces—and simultaneously invents—his
own subjective limit, while Heloise is left to point, via her unfinished
sentence, to her continued existence beyond the story's frame.

As in Antonioni's *temps morts*, the tension Carson renders apparent here, between the lived moment (however scripted) and the
unscripted expanse beyond, points to the continuity rather than the
disjunction between presence and absence, as between consciousness
and what exceeds conscious apprehension. The dash that follows
Heloise's unfinished question is not an empty gesture. It is, instead,
an effort to extend the utterance beyond the embodied experience of
the subject or "actor" on the stage. Like one of Sappho's fragments,
which Carson includes in the title section of *Decreation*, the words
are charged with their own ending, with the fact that they "break off,"
that we "don't know where [they are] headed from here."

As Carson points out in relation to Sappho's poem, what we see is
the "turn toward" that unknown content, toward its "unreachable goal":

And cold sweat holds me and shaking
Grips me all, greener than grass
I am and dead—or almost
I seem to me

But all is to be dared, because even a person of poverty…

Here, at the end of the fragment, grammar breaks down. The personal pronouns, confused, turn inward to address and, finally, "undo" the poem. Past simple being ("I am") and the supplement of death; past the gesture of writing and its attempt (a simple stroke across the page "—") to bridge the divide between what "is" (simple being) and what is "not yet" (the supplement of death); past uncertainty; past the subjective territory of seems, "all" is still "to be dared."

Writing is the inscription of this absolute potential and, as such, it acts as a medium for what, beyond the finite framework of subjectivity and the individuated body, persists in and as that absolute. For Woolf, writing and language had the capacity to transcribe the waves of human consciousness; for Carson, it has the capacity to transcribe silence and what remains unscripted and unknown. Both authors strive through their writing to disrupt and ultimately dissolve the border between inside and outside, life and death. In their works, both subject and language falter and break down, but they are never negated. Disjunction, blank space, and absence function not as means to deny or evade meaning, but instead work to clear and hold place for the supplement, for "truth." An always necessarily imaginary and projected plenitude—a plenitude that will fulfill itself only in the "last moment"—is thus revealed in, and as, the fundamental content of the work.

When F. H. Myers died, William James sought to transcribe a message from his friend from beyond the grave, but, in the end, he was confronted with an empty page. What this encounter, like much of Carson's and Woolf's work, illustrates is that, although subjective experience and its transcription may never objectively transcend the limits of the body or the page, nor express what is quite literally beyond them, they may nevertheless be activated as a point of receptivity and as a negative figuration of this *beyond*. It is, in other words, precisely through an encounter with the limitations of language, the body, and the private mind that we render apparent the point of contact between inside and outside, self and other, and begin to recognize and potentially employ both language and the body as vehicles of inspiration—of the "in and out of substantial breath."

"Poetic Emergency"
George Oppen's Political and Poetical Thinking

Defining himself against earlier Imagist poetry, George Oppen rejected what he saw as a too-easy faith in the visual. Along with other poets of his generation associated with the "Objectivist" movement—Charles Reznikoff, Louis Zukofsky, Lorine Niedecker, and Carl Rakosi—Oppen was concerned with the materiality of objects, language, and perception, but only insofar as material forms could give access to, or provide expression for, what subtends them. "Over what," he asks in a poem included in his earliest collection, *Discrete Series*, "has the air frozen?" With this question, Oppen establishes the manner in which he will attempt, throughout his career, to render even the most intangible of elements solid. The air is objectified—"frozen"—in order to point to the possibility of a further intangibility just beyond the limits of the poet's language and imagination.

Language, for Oppen, exists in a similarly suspended state—hovering above the fugitive and immaterial experiences it seeks to name. He believed that by revealing the objective limits of language, the poetic process was able to articulate what language could not.

"I look for the thinnest possible surface," Oppen wrote in a letter to Cid Corman from 1960, "– – at times, no doubt too thin: a hole, a lapse…There is no point in defending lapses – – but that is, of all risks the one I plan to live with. I am much more afraid of a solid mass of words." As Oppen intimates, it is precisely in the moments when language seems to falter that, in his own estimation, he succeeds as a poet. Already in his early poetry, but still more overtly in later work, Oppen came to rely on the "holes" or silences both within and at the limit of language as a means of directing the reader beyond the objective confines of each poem.

Oppen's most famous "lapse"—which he may or may not have been alluding to in his letter to Corman—was the twenty-five-year period following the 1934 publication of *Discrete Series* during which he wrote no poetry at all. For Oppen, any poem that tied itself to "a moral or a political (same thing) judgement" was essentially "bad"; poetry and politics served separate purposes and existed, necessarily, in separate spheres. In the 1930s, Oppen and his wife, Mary, threw themselves into their work for the Communist Party and the Workers Alliance of America. Oppen fought in World War II and was seriously wounded. After the war, he relocated his family to Mexico, where they lived during the McCarthy era as political exiles. In this quarter-century, he chose to "risk" silence over what he saw as the greater risk of writing "bad poetry."

Following the family's return to the United States in 1958, Oppen's decision to return to poetry signalled a change in his thinking about the relation between poetry and politics. Both during the "lapse" in his writing career and after, Oppen was, undeniably, influenced by a consistent, though shifting, engagement with political action and thought. When he returned to writing, it was—as Peter Nicholls has observed—poetry's ability to emphasize (even through its failure) the "irreducibility of experience to knowledge" that Oppen identified as a potential source of "generative opacity within political thinking."

"Poetry," wrote Oppen in a letter to his sister June dated 1959, "has to be protean; the meaning must begin there…A poem has got to be written into the future. I don't mean something about the admiration of posterity (from where I sit, posterity looks like a bunch of damn kids) but simply that it's something that is not the past." As with the unknown element over which the air seems to have "frozen" in his early poem, here Oppen depicts the future in the negative—conceptualized as that which exceeds the limit of what can be positively known. Oppen's late work demonstrates this conscientious turn away from an engagement with the present, with what apparently "is," in an effort to confront this inconceivable future. "I…returned to poetry only when we knew that we had failed," he remarked once, in reference to his political activity previous to, and directly following, the war (quoted by Nicholls). And yet, "failure" marks a point of departure for Oppen: the beginning of what Michael Palmer would, in the 1980s, call *trust*—"a trust to a kind of errancy, which is also an erring, making errors" (quoted in Thomas Gardner's *Regions of Unlikeness*).

In *The End of the Poem*, Giorgio Agamben defines poetry as a "schism of sound and sense." There is, he explains, an inherent disjunction between the "semiotic event" of the poem (that is, the event of language itself, its objective presence on the page, its sound) and the "semantic event"—the poem's meaning. Echoing Oppen's remark that poetry "has to be protean," Agamben argues that the continued oscillation between sound and sense in a poem results in a state of perpetual "poetic emergency." It is, he explains, precisely at the point in which "sound is about to be ruined in the abyss of sense," or vice versa, that the poem—at least conceptually—"suspend(s) its own end."

Even when the *actual* end of the poem arrives, then, the poem continues to sustain itself through its reverberations. By directing the reader or listener beyond the apprehension of content to the relation between sound and sense, sound and silence, the poem's material or sensible end marks a point of "poetic emergency" where language, liberated from its commitment to meaning, becomes autonomous—able to, as Agamben writes, "communicate itself." The end of the poem marks a space of "failure" in Oppen's sense: it exists as a zone of openness and potentiality in the negative space that surrounds and subtends objective language.

Oppen shares Agamben's sense that poetic language should ideally effect an "exact coincidence between sense and sound," such that the poem would appear fully, "without remaining unsaid in what is said." This is made plain in another letter to Cid Corman from 1960 in which Oppen writes: "The problem of diction seems to me that the poem must contain its words entirely." This total manifestation is—as Agamben admits—a "poetic impossibility," but it is also the poem's defining structure. It is *not*, after all, Agamben claims, through the language of a poem that a poem ultimately communicates; instead, poetic meaning is transmitted by evoking the schism between language and the objective world.

Oppen's later work demonstrates this. In a poem included in his second collection, *The Materials* (1962), Oppen juxtaposes, mixes, and undercuts the distance between language, self, and world in order to arrive at a moment of rupture between being and the discourse of being that—paradoxically—communicates a sense of fulfillment and plenitude:

> Returning to that house
> And the rounded rocks of childhood – They have lasted
> well.
>
> A world of things.
>
> An aging man,
> The knuckles of my hand
> So jointed! I am this?

In the poem's final line, with its wonderful moment of split recognition/non-recognition of self—"So jointed! I am this?"—Oppen realizes the "poetic impossibility" of marrying sense and sound, as he articulates both a sensual and sensible awareness of the material body through the semantic event of the poem.

Owing largely, no doubt, to a developing interest in Martin Heiddegger's thinking, Oppen's later collections are preoccupied by the desire, already evident in *Discrete Series*, to render tangible that which extends beyond the limits of physical "perceptions" and "the world of things." Or, conversely, his later works manifest a desire to extend that "world of things" to include all that is potentially (emotionally *or* physically) perceivable to the subject. Sometimes stumblingly, his poetry seeks to evoke being not through a process of naming or description but through a "disclosure of being" at the moment of being: as Nicholls puts it, "a 'letting-be' of 'what-is.'"

"Even the New Englander," writes Oppen in "Product," another poem included in *The Materials*, "was boatness." As this recourse to a neologism indicates, standard vocabulary often fails us, revealing the gap between words and what they seek to describe, as well as, more fundamentally, between description and being. For Oppen, poetry takes place in this gap—in the process of recognizing the material of the poem as a fallible body ("So jointed! I am this?"). The poem discloses this moment of recognition as a complex interplay between the material and the immaterial, or between what can and cannot be expressed through words. It is important to Oppen that this process remain active—situated within the subjective experience of the poet as he struggles against the limits of both his language and his world. Because of this, Oppen's return to poetry after a twenty-five-year silence should be read not as a personal vindication of an aesthetic or disciplinary category, but as a renewed trust in the errant *process* of poetry—which is to say, in *poiesis*.

Unlike Heidegger, who posited poetry as more "authentic" and therefore as essentially superior to other modes of knowing,[1] Oppen continued to resist poetry even after he went back to writing it. To write a poem continued to be, for him, the articulation of an impossible dilemma rather than the pursuit of a realizable goal. His practice, in this sense, can be understood as a form of resistance to the dangers of totalizing thought—dangers that Heidegger's political thinking of the 1930s and 1940s illustrates all too clearly.

In *The End of the Poem*, Agamben observes that when philosophy or political thinking acts "as if sound and sense coincided," they run the risk of "falling into banality." Recalling Wittgenstein's notion that, to avoid such banality, "philosophy should really only be poeticized," Agamben avers that poetry "should really only be philosophized." Working within and against the inherent tension between sense and sound in discourse, poetry "suspends the end" of thought and language by demonstrating the inability of both to either fully resist or fully resolve themselves in meaning. For Oppen, this resistance affords a way of confronting and addressing symbolic language. Language itself becomes "other" and, rather than simply oscillating between sense and sound, an uncanny space is opened *between* them—between, that is, language as a vehicle for subjective meaning and language as a material and/or sensual object.

Always "one inch above, one inch below what has already been said"—Oppen wrote in a letter to Michael Heller in 1972—"the world opens up." For Oppen, language served as a site of specific, material engagement, but while he emphasized the fact of language on the page, he also called attention to its thinness—drawing it like a sheet of ice over what refused to be named. In so doing, Oppen's poems indicate the very real presence and proximity of what is not, or not-yet, language. Poetry, as these poems demonstrate, is not a form but a protean process in which language—crossing with and touching upon the unsaid—no longer needs to be spoken for because it "communicate(s) itself."

"If we dare to"

Border Crossings in Erín Moure's *O Cidadán*

Poetry at this time, I believe, has the capacity and perhaps
the obligation to enter those specific zones known as
borders, since borders are by definition addressed to
foreignness, and in a complex sense, best captured in
another Greek word, *xenos*. It, too, means "stranger,"
or "foreigner"…In using the metaphor of a border, I do
not mean to suggest that poetry relegate itself to the
margins. The border is not an edge along the fringe of
society and experience but rather their very middle—their
between; it names the condition of doubt and encounter
which being foreign to a situation (which may be life
itself) provokes—a condition which is simultaneously
an impasse and a passage, limbo and transit zone…

—Lyn Hejinian

Erín Moure's 2002 collection, *O Cidadán*, is an invitation into the "middle" of language. It deliberately draws attention to the borders between different languages, as well as to those between language and not language, language and silence, in order to illustrate that these borders are as much internal to language and selfhood as they are external. They are always, therefore, in the process of being transgressed.

In *My Beloved Wager*, a collection of essays published seven years after *O Cidadán*, Moure reflects: "To nurture languages is to create localization not in soil but in events, for it is, strangely, events that enact localities, no site can pre-exist some event's *act*." With *O Cidadán*, Moure brings disparate languages or approaches to language into contact specifically so that they might enact locality in an *actual* rather than a geographical sense. The text's main language—English—becomes a space of "doubt and encounter" as it collides with, and is intersected by, French, Castilian, Galician, Latin, Portuguese, and the blank space of the page. *Cidadán*, for example, is the Galician word for *citizen*, but Moure's poetic exploration of the term troubles the possibility of direct translation. She presents the intertwinings of its multiple meanings through linguistic and typographical experimentation with the aim of establishing the abstract concept of the citizen-subject as a body with borders. Simultaneously, she posits language and thought as a way of "touching," and even crossing, those lines.

By rendering these crossings between embodied subjects visible on the page, Moure exposes the citizen—like the language that describes or delimits the citizen—as an act that complicates, blurs, and makes strange the experience of a fixed subject position. In an essay included in *My Beloved Wager*, Moure emphasizes the manner in which the subject is constructed through its embodiment and its performative relation to others:

> I, facing you, whom I do not know, admit that *you* have some prior claim on me, one that preceded and enables the creation of my *self*...And one of us can never be subsumed in the other, colonized, explained. Our relationship is gestural. Genuflectual. Proximal. The paradox of the construction of the self (which is, as Judith Butler says, performative) is a microcosm of the paradox of the construction of a nation, of nacionalidade.

O Cidadán enacts this observation by demonstrating that the paradox of the construction of language is a microcosm of both the paradox of nationhood and the paradox of self. Even the simplest language event presupposes a "facing you" that creates both the possibility of and an object for language. Although the speaker's language necessarily remains at a distance and/or "foreign" to the "other" of address and is not guaranteed a response, every address depends upon the possibility of its being heard, i.e., upon the speaker's relation to an outside "other" who—whether they are listening or not—enjoys a "prior claim" over the speech event.

It is easy to see how this relationship, understood at the level of the subject, can be assimilated into a hegemonic power structure. In *O Cidadán*, Moure challenges this potential assimilation by redirecting, overturning, and obscuring any simplistic or one-sided textual interpretations: elongated rectangles cover sections of the text, concealing some words and leaving others exposed; blank spaces fragment otherwise coherent phrases; graphs chart the multiple relationships between individual words; arrows direct the reader's attention to other sections of the text; the writings of St. Augustine, Jacques Derrida, Emmanuel Levinas, and Jean-Luc Nancy intertwine with the speaker's own thoughts; Spanish, Galician, and French words are left untranslated alongside the English; "notes" toward the manuscript's potential revision are included—for example, the penultimate line of "document 29," which reads, "(add pp.120-121 Nancy here)."

All of these strategies reveal the text as a site of flux and the "borders" of language and selfhood as liminal spaces that actively *resist* rather than enforce definition. They gesture—like the excerpt from Nancy that is not actually provided—toward what helped to shape the text by bordering it, by remaining *outside* or on the edge.[1] What Moure's project ultimately serves to illustrate, then, is that the "outside" is also *inside*, at the "very middle." What is experienced at one level as an omission (ready meaning, fully legible text, or pages 120–121 of a Nancy text) is also shown to quite literally shape the page.

Moure's exploration of the complex relationship between outside and inside at this "microcosmic" level of the text allows her to reflect on parallel complexities at the level of nationhood and the self. She further suggests that a confrontation with a border zone at *any* of these levels—text, self, nation—is inseparable from a confrontation with often invisible structures of power.

In her 1990 article "Arts of the Contact Zone," Mary Louise Pratt studies border confrontations using the story of Felipe Guaman Pomo, an Indigenous Andean whose seventeenth-century *Nueva Corónica* constituted a syncretic account of Indigenous and Christian histories. The work can be classified as an autoethnographic text, which Pratt defines as one in which a person or people "undertake(s) to describe themselves in ways that engage with representations others have made of them." This active process of rewriting allows for some reallocation of power, but the problem of the dialogue's ultimate one-sidedness remains. As Pratt makes clear with the example of Pomo's text, which has remained virtually unread, "miscomprehension, incomprehension, dead letters, unread masterpieces, absolute heterogeneity of meaning—these are some of the perils of writing in the contact zone."

Moure's *O Cidadán* illustrates the ways in which "miscomprehension" and "incomprehension" can be employed poetically to transmit multiple possible interpretive events rather than to obscure or block a single meaning. She establishes a "contact zone" wherein her own processes of reading, thinking, and writing about language and identity intersect with the thinking of dominant critical theorists and language philosophers. By engaging these theorists without either adopting or rejecting their points of view, Moure exposes the "prior claim" her reading life has over her writing life and underlines the fundamental relation within every instance of language and being between creativity and receptivity, self and other.

The inclusion of outside texts and untranslated non-English words in Moure's text also foregrounds the active and ongoing interpretive process that constitutes both language and identity. The "Substitution of Harms" sequence in *O Cidadán* illustrates this active process by representing the relationship between language and meaning as a series of mathematical fractions:

$$\frac{\text{Harm}}{\text{Forms}} \quad \frac{\text{harm}}{\text{term}} \quad \frac{\text{harm}}{\text{devices}} \sqrt{} \quad \frac{\text{harm}}{\text{units}} \quad \frac{\text{harm}}{\text{count.}}$$

Moure refers to these figures as "catalogues," but what they emphasize is the impossibility of ever exhaustively "cataloguing"

anything. The poem sequence purposely withholds direct signification and instead reveals the literal gaps or openings between signifier
and signified, and thus, the continuously shifting relation between
signs. Nevertheless, the sequence still manages to be *significant*, gen-
eratively evoking the way that words combine and, in making or
failing to make contact with one another, become both agents and
beneficiaries of meaning.

In "document 2" of *O Cidadán*, Moure explores this shifting
ground of signification through the concept of the body—a concept
she arrives at by reading, and sharing, the writings of Nancy. Citing
Nancy's description of *sense* as a "touching at the confines of the
world," Moure asks, "How to write the sense of the world?" Nothing,
Nancy posits, can exist "in itself," but instead only in relation to itself
and to the world onto which it "opens." "The *différance* of the
toward-itself," he writes, "in accordance with which sense opens, is
inscribed *along the edge of* the 'in itself.' *Corpus:* all bodies, each outside the others, make up the inorganic body of the sense." In her own
text, Moure employs the term *body* in the same broad sense as Nancy.
She uses it variously, sometimes to denote the physical human body,
sometimes to denote a solid object of any description, and sometimes
to ground an abstract or theoretical relationship in concrete terms.

In "document 2," we encounter all of these potential meanings.
"The cidadán stands in time as the person stands in space," writes
Moure, "liquid / edge before or beyond the other she craves, the she
she craves also a she, / and this is space that opens time…" Intro-
duced first is the theoretic body: "The cidadán" portrayed as a
linguistic abstraction—"nothing to do with country or / origin."
Next, we encounter the physical body, understood objectively as "the
person," "the other." Finally, we are presented with the embodied
subject: "the she she craves also a she." In this context, the emphasis
on the "she she craves" being "also a she" serves not only to signify
the speaker's subjectivity in terms of gender and sexual orientation, it

also enacts the process of self-identification—the word "also" pointing to the speaker's realization that "she" (herself) is also a "she" and that she therefore exists both inside (as "I") and out (as someone else's "she").

In "document 7," Moure continues to explore the relationship between "outside" and "inside" in the creation of selfhood through a meditation on the act of reading. Having determined that "the origin of any particular condensation of meaning is…outside the body," the speaker reflects on the fact that such a determination "beckons the whole notion of 'outside' into the field of inquiry and / unseats it. For…what is 'inside'? What is 'in' that must be kept 'in' / so badly that 'outside' must be denominated as function?"

Thoughtful and engaged reading, Moure suggests, is a way of redefining the borders between self and other, inside and out. In an essay titled "Reading Never Ceases to Amaze Me," Moure explicitly argues that reading affords us the opportunity to see "where self is constructed, recognizing where thought's wires act as stop signs," as well as the possibility of "learning to walk past those wires, learning that the borders in one's thought are but seams." Reading is "where thought risks," Moure asserts. "And more: reading is where thought risks concatenation with that which is exterior to it."

In *O Cidadán*, Moure makes borders visible (for example, by drawing a dotted line around a text that deliberately runs past the boundary the line suggests), not to emphasize the inevitability of limits or ruptures, but to reframe those limits as connective tissue— as mutually supporting overlaps that constitute notions of selfhood and other *from within*. This recognition of the imbrication of inside and outside allows us to see the ways in which we affect change imminently. If there is to be any change at a social and political level, that change will be deeply connected with shifts in thinking at a personal or private level.

This is an idea explicitly explored in *Furious*—a collection for which Moure won the Governor General's Award for poetry in 1988. To make "women's speaking possible," it is not "the weight and force of English" that needs to be changed, Moure writes in this collection; what is needed, instead, is to "move the force in any language, create a slippage, even for a moment…to decentre the 'thing,' unmask the relation." Susan Rudy observes that Moure achieves this goal within her own work by writing, purposely, "in excess of signification"—subverting conventional word usage and redeploying grammar, punctuation, syntax, and spelling. The "slippage" that results between word and meaning may be momentary, but it nonetheless produces lasting effects. "Once we've crossed a border," Moure writes, "we can't expect the border to remain the same. It is marked by our passage."

Ultimately, Moure, like Pratt, is interested not in eradicating borders but in recognizing the very real and concrete implications of where, when, and why we draw certain lines—and who is permitted to draw and to cross them. The figure of the *cidadán* thus becomes an invitation to think transgressively—but, importantly, not transcendentally—about the contiguities between subjective experience, conceptions of identity, national histories, and language, while also acknowledging the position of privilege enjoyed by anyone who (like the author) is capable of *thinking* about borders while crossing them.

Moure's interest in both the implicit and explicit effects of linguistic and national borders is shaped by this privilege—as well as by her experience outside of the majority culture of the places in and of which she writes (Galicia, Spain, and Montreal, Quebec). Hers is a "minor literature" in Deleuze and Guattari's sense,[2] and yet the terms *major* and *minor* lend a falsely hierarchical notion to the interplay between languages in Moure's work, as well as to their relationship both to nationality and selfhood. Rather than theoretically refer to linguistic, cultural, or personal juxtapositions, Moure seeks to localize these juxtapositions—to represent different experiences of language and identity spatially as "zones that can overlap"—and, in doing so, to call into question binary notions of exteriority and interiority, major and minor, self and other.

Inevitably, however, the effort to subvert binary notions is also an engagement with and a representation of those binaries. Moure's figuration of the relation between words as fractal, for example, unavoidably introduces the idea of an *original* word that can be divided or "split." Moure is conscious and self-reflexive about the issues her poetic strategies introduce. At the bottom of "Second Catalogue of the Substitution of Harms," a note reads: "*in the form of ~~functions~~ fractions*," a reference to the *sous-rature* or "under-erasure" method developed by Heidegger and later employed by deconstructionist thinkers like Derrida.

For Derrida, placing text under erasure created the possibility "of a discourse which borrows from a heritage the resources necessary for the deconstruction of that heritage." Moure's borrowing from deconstructionist methods provides both her and her readers the resources necessary to critique and destabilize the theoretical framework from which she borrows; for example, in emphasizing the material effects of these methods on the page, her work manifests an implicit critique of a primarily theoretical approach to deconstruction. The typographical experimentations and illustrative components of *O Cidadán* serve to challenge the idea of "origin" and propose an interplay between the many possible meanings of any given word or arrangement of words, but they do so by creating an almost comically tangible, rather than abstract or regressive, space of encounter between the various voices and texts on the page (think Charlie Chaplin tripping over the line with which a concept is placed *sous rature*).

"Touching is the very experience of 'origin' as 'plural singularity,'" writes Derrida in *On Touching*. In order to exist and/or be perceived at all, that is, a body must already exist in relation both to itself and to the world. And yet, at the same time, a body—like a mark on a page—exists contiguously and, as Moure writes, "without absorption." Moure reflects: "Is there an originary marking? If there were, would we be able to 'read' it at all? Or does such a 'trait' receive its function as mark only from our reading, our imposition of acculturated being that takes place in reading's gesture. And is thereby not originary." Although Moure echoes the manner in which Derrida, Nancy, and other deconstructionists problematize the notion of "origin," she also strives to incorporate the "abstract" value of the idea of origin by figuring the relationship between language and meaning in personal, as well as spatial, terms. Later on in the same poem, she asserts: "already my reading is what creates / it as 'trait,' no? / Therefore, 'not originary.'"

When it comes to specifically exploring the process of translation, Moure succeeds in turning the idea of an "original language" inside out, exposing our experience of what *feels* original as a "contact zone" of multiple experiences, histories, and possible articulations. In "document 29 (French thinking)," she observes: "To enable a language (returning) is also to allow intrusion, and to enable / intrusions or their possibility as part of the cultural order. An overlay (micro) / into a zone." In this part of the poem, Moure emphasizes the way that languages impinge on each other and that cultural histories are created in the spaces of contact and interplay between different peoples, traditions, and patterns of thinking. A little later, in the same poem, she writes: "My thinking, because of (necessary) zone disequilibrium, may be / 'French' thinking, even in English."

Moure's suggestion that her own thinking is inflected with what Derrida refers to as "a French tradition" of reflexiveness, as well as "of a certain problematic of touch," once again draws attention to the borders between languages and experiences of language that, often invisibly, delimit our identities and our understandings of the world.

By self-reflexively considering her own thinking as an amalgamation of different languages and traditions, she represents thought and identity as embodied structures that can be added to, intersected with, and changed.

"Sometimes only the 'overlap' makes borders of a zone visible," Moure reminds us. By acknowledging the borders between languages, identities, and ways of thinking, we are better able to conceive of the ways we touch and are touched by others. It is in demonstrating her *awareness* of her own "French thinking" that, for example, Moure is able in O Cidadán to displace and, in effect, change English. Our subjective identities and experiences are, the work suggests, constantly being shaped and reshaped by what we encounter outside of us, and "take in"; conversely, it is an inward shift in thinking that brings about outward change. Nancy describes "a philosophy of confines" and asserts that, because we can never "occupy the originary point" of any perspective, we "touch our limits from all sides." Moure enacts this philosophy as a poetic event, grounding her own investigation into the taking place of being and language in an exploration, and demonstration, of the limits of the poetic text. Although this method risks flattening the infinite, multidirectional concept of selfhood Nancy proposes into language, Moure avoids this reduction by pointing toward what Nancy calls the multidirectional "spacious space" inherent within all linguistic representation. Language is "[n]ot 'dualistic' but 'mesial'" she writes.

The word *mesial*, which denotes a movement toward the middle line of a body, complicates a "philosophy of confines" in that it requires us to imagine the experience of touching as one "confined" by an interior rather than exterior boundary. It is the body, or text, Moure suggests—not the world that body or text opens onto or "touches" upon—that acts as a limit. Recognizing the body/text as structured by and inherently connected to what exceeds it is thus a strategy for exceeding perceived limits.

In "document 7 (outside)," Moure asks: "if the trait falls *outside* of the body or bodies of both, what is 'inside'?" Moure repeats this question frequently and variously throughout this work, both through her language and through illustrative figures on the page. For example, the text that spills across its text block in "Twentieth Century of the Festering of Harms" asks this question in visual form—as does the interruption of "document 21 (a chuvia no peito)" by an illustration of a set of lungs, the placing under erasure of the words "Sweet catalpa, Frederico" in "My Volition's Faint Trill," and the addition of a note at the bottom of "document 29 (French thinking)": "This piece ends with a list of email addresses of friends in Chile and Spain." By rendering visible its perceived bounds and risking contact with what exceeds it, the body/text explodes the dichotomy of inside and out and expresses itself as an inexhaustible set of possible relations—while still acknowledging its obligation to social, political, and cultural influences and constraints.

Both poetic and political, abstract and corporeal, Moure's *cidadán* becomes just this sort of risky textual body. It exists as "a prosthetic gesture (across 'languages')," but also, ultimately, across the conceptual divide between "subject" and "citizen." The *cidadán* has "nothing to do with country or origin" and "stands in time as the person stands in space." She is a citizen in Nancy's sense: "first of all, *one, some*one, *everyone*," encompassing "numerous unicities." Rather than a projected ideal, the *cidadán* is a figure through which to explore the subject, and the subject's language, as inherently committed. The space of the self, Moure indicates, like the space of a poem, is not only a means of "becoming"; it already *exists*, and in existing, is indissociable from being-embodied.

To be a subject is, necessarily, to be a citizen, and the city or state—in that it is made up of citizen-subjects—"has no identity other than the space in which citizens cross each other's paths," writes Nancy. Moure's text is a mapping of this border landscape, which, "like a dream landscape," is shifting, uncertain, "perpetually incomplete" (Lynn Hejinian in *The Language of Inquiry*), but also dependent upon a dreaming body. This relationship between the ideal and the real is "not dualistic but mesial." It is a space of continual movement where not only disparate languages and cultures, but also our disparate experiences of language and culture, intersect with one another, and "touch." In directing us toward the body as a locus of connection and meaning-making, *O Cidadán* is an invitation to recognize both language and selfhood as embodied "contact zones," and sites of change. "Poetry," Moure reminds us, "is a limitless genre. Its borders are only in ourselves and we can move them, in our lifetimes, if we dare to."

Visual Histories

Metzger, Paterson, and the
Cartography of Lyric Time

"With how many things are we on the brink of
becoming acquainted, if cowardice or careless-
ness did not restrain our inquiries."
—Mary Shelley, *Frankenstein*

During a series of twenty-minute sessions, an EEG depicted the electrical activity occurring in artist and political activist Gustav Metzger's brain as he attempted to think about nothing.[1] Using this data as a set of instructions, a robot then proceeded to carve a corresponding negative shape into the interior of a fifty-centimetre cube of 145 million-year-old fossilized Portland stone. The result is *Null Object*, an installation by London Fieldworks (Bruce Gilchrist and Jo Joelson) from 2012.

In two related projects from 2007, multidisciplinary artist Katie Paterson similarly explores the contingent relation between the time-bound subject and objective records of deep time. One such project, *Langjökull, Snæfellsjökull, Solheimajökull*, involved making sound recordings of three Icelandic glaciers that were then cast into record form using the meltwater from each glacier. The recordings were played simultaneously on three turntables, the sound of the melting glaciers intermingling with the sound of the melting records (see Katiepaterson.org). In the second project, *Vatnajökull (the sound of)*, Paterson placed a microphone lead into an outlet lagoon near the Vatnajökull glacier. Connected to an amplifier and a mobile phone, the microphone had the potential to transmit the sound of the melting glacier to any caller in the world.

By figuring an imagined discursive space or "I-thou relation" between a speaking subject and a natural object, all three of these projects can be approached as maps, or models, of the poetic act. Each project renders palpable the way that poetic address makes nothing quite literally *happen*[2] through the representation of what Jonathan Culler calls a "voice-event," which hollows out the subject and displaces narrative time.

As Culler notes in *Theory of the Lyric*, what the apostrophic relation establishes is not "the description and interpretation of a past event" but "the iterative and iterable performance of an event in the lyric present, in the special 'now,' of lyric articulation." In presenting a literal inscription of subjective experience within and as a natural object, London Fieldworks' *Null Object* and Paterson's glacier works evoke the slippery and often dissonant relationship between human and non-human historical records and time-scales. They provide a tangible and/or audible representation of the possibility of addressing time itself from the limited framework of human perspective. What's more, they create the material conditions for a response to that address. This is most clearly and directly perceptible in the case of Vatnajökull's mobile phone number (+44(0)7757001122), which presents us with both the opportunity to literally *call* a 2,500-year-old glacier and the sensory experience of the glacier's response.

Null Object and *Langjökull, Snæfellsjökull, Solheimajökull* present a more complicated relationship between subjective call and objective response, but in both cases a conceptual space of contact is established between the limited framework of the subject and deep time. Where *Null Object* can be understood as a snapshot of Metzger's address to the limits of his own subjectivity—through his attempt to think about nothing, his engagement with a technology that figures that attempt, and the juxtaposition of that figuration against fossilized stone—Paterson's *Langjökull, Snæfellsjökull, Solheimajökull* both communicates the response of glacial meltwater to changing conditions over time and serves as a literal record of the past.

All three projects offer material figurations of the way that "voice-events," produced through the address to non-human objects, serve to suspend the limitations of time-bound subjective experience precisely by confronting, and thereby confirming, that limit. Like Mary Shelley's Doctor Frankenstein, who—wandering in another glacial landscape—comes face to face with an embodiment of his personal limitations in the form of a creature he himself has created, these projects evoke the ambiguous and contingent relation between subject and object, human and non-human.

A creature who can "exist in the ice caves of the glaciers and hide himself from pursuit among the ridges of inaccessible precipices" is a being, Doctor Frankenstein reasons, "possessing faculties it would be vain to cope with." Feeling the restrictions of his individual agency even over the product of his own imagination, he cries out: "Oh! Stars and clouds and winds, ye are all about to mock me!" This address to what exists profoundly beyond a subjective framework serves to simultaneously accentuate and eliminate the distance between the doctor's individual being and the natural world. "If ye really pity me, crush sensation and memory," he continues, "let me become as nought; but if not, depart, depart, and leave me in darkness."

Null Object and Paterson's glacier works illustrate the paradox of poetic address Shelley's passage evokes—palpably demonstrating that what results from poetic communication is not a causal relation between (finite) speaker and (the infinite) addressed but instead, a contingent "voice-event." The speaker, in other words, does not and cannot erode the causal and material structures of space and time according to which a subject takes place and understands itself as a subject. However, in being brought into proximity through the process of address, the poetic act establishes a dislocated, atemporal space (Culler's "special 'now'"), in which a reader or interpreter is invited to confront, if not infinity—that is, the absolute in itself— then the absolute *contingency* of the time-bound subject on what infinitely exceeds it.[3]

Doctor Frankenstein's address to the universe, for example—"let me become as nought; but if not, depart, depart, and leave me in darkness"—makes "nothing happen" by inviting the reader or listener to participate in a performative "voice-event." The layering of negatives in this particular address works to disrupt binary oppositions between presence and absence, self and other, cause and effect. The address itself stages a confrontation with "nothing" that dislocates causal and temporal flow and establishes what Culler calls a "triangulated" space of lyric encounter.

"Triangulated" address, which moves between a speaker, an (often absent) addressee, and a reader or listener, is, Culler writes, "the root-form of presentation for lyric" and the basis of all lyric poems, regardless of whether they make overt use of special modes of address such as apostrophe. Excised from a linear temporal trajectory, lyric form resists the subordination of language to interpretation, affect to effect, revolutionary possibility to historical determinism[4]—in short, every possible representation. It is the representation of this lyric *resistance* to representation—to the reifying forces of history and meaning—that allows both London Fieldworks and Paterson to present the confrontation between finite subjectivity and the infinite, evoking what Walter Benjamin calls a "unique experience" of deep time as it "flashes up at a moment of danger."

Benjamin's elliptical "Theses on the Philosophy of History," which counters the imposition of an "eternal" image of the past with the possibilities afforded by individual experience and memory, can perhaps best be understood through the lens of Culler's theory of lyric address. Rather than a linear progression from past to future in which the present is just a momentary stop along the way, Benjamin argues that each moment emerges due only to "a secret agreement between past generations and the present one," in which the past has agency and the past, present, and future exist contingently and contiguously, in constant dialogue.

Time and history are not linear in structure, in other words, but lyric. Excised from the flow of value and interpretation, what occurs—and reoccurs, continually—is the relation between subjectivity and objectivity, contingent possibility and a constantly reconfiguring set of material conditions. Both London Fieldwork's *Null Object* and Paterson's glacier works represent this relation, evoking both the revolutionary "promise" of radical interruption and change inherent within each moment and the implicit possibility that this promise will remain unrealized, bounded by the material conditions according to which it has been generated: "an act of radical interiorization and solipsism," in Culler's words.

By providing a three-dimensional and/or experiential model of the poetic act, however, London Fieldworks and Paterson interrupt a solipsistic understanding of the relation between "subject" and "object," human and non-human. Rather than translating the distance between human and non-human into, on the one hand, a sublime experience of Nature or, on the other, a neo-liberal discussion about the environment's "value" and "costs," these artists ask us to recognize the irreducible difference between subjective, finite frameworks of space and time—including the subject's perceptions of "difference" itself, i.e., what it means to be "a subject"—and what exceeds every frame. As in Doctor Frankenstein's address to the "stars and clouds and winds," this tension between subject and object, human and non-human, is made palpable through juxtaposition and the illustration of distance: presence announced via reference to potential absence, the possibility of encounter charted via the triangulation of specific points of departure. What these configurations reveal is that the poetic act takes place not as a realizable "thing" but, instead, as precisely *nothing*. The poetic act can only be read, that is, in the negative, against that which exceeds it: as, for example, the null shape of Metzger's thinking about nothing, or as the vanishing record of glacial time.

This, then, is what poetry offers: the opportunity to conceive of time not as causal or linear—each moment a site for potential progress, a "stop along the way"—but instead as a unique experience between subject and object, concept and form. To engage in a poetic act by seriously confronting the limits of human perspective is to expand our sense of the potential ambit of acquaintance and relation. It is also to afford agency to the deep past in relation to the present, the abstract ideal in relation to its material conditions, and the finite moment in relation to the infinite movement of time.

A "Most Human" Call

Responding to Muriel Rukeyser's *The Life of Poetry*

"A poem does invite, it does require," wrote Rukeyser in her book of collected essays, *The Life of Poetry*, first published in 1949. "What does it invite? A poem invites you to feel. More than that: it invites you to respond. And better than that: a poem invites a total response." Rather than treating experience "fact by fact, deriving the connections," poetry, she writes, reveals and explores "relationships themselves, learning the facts as they feed and destroy each other."

Rukeyser does not limit her conception of poetry to the "literary arts" or its products, but instead, as the title of her book implies, she considers poetry a vital entity: a dynamic and self-reflexive way of perceiving and responding to the world. It is precisely the totality of poetry's invited response, Rukeyser suggests—its emotional as well as intellectual expression—that often inspires fear of, and even "direct resistance" to, poetry. But were we able to actually *live* in the manner that poetry invites—"in full response to the earth, to each other, and to ourselves"—we might, she challenges us, "be more human."[1]

It was in order to meet this challenge that Rukeyser sought a "new definition of what a poem might be." In 1936, at the age of twenty-two, Rukeyser had just returned from a stint overseas, reporting from Barcelona on the People's Olympiad and the outbreak of the Spanish Civil War. Disturbed by the reports she heard of the situation in Gauley Bridge, West Virginia, she set off to investigate what is recognized today as one of the worst industrial disasters in American history—a labour catastrophe in which hundreds to thousands of miners died from lung disease caused by breathing silica dust, as Catherine Venable Moore records. In 1938, Rukeyser practised her "new definition" of poetry in the long poetic sequence "The Book of the Dead," published in the collection *US1*. By incorporating documentary elements (interview transcripts, excerpts from letters, statistical charts) into the sequence, Rukeyser emphasized the rifts and continuities between the journalistic facts of the Hawks Nest Tunnel Disaster and a poetic structure dedicated to the idea of living and writing in "full response" to those facts, and to the larger reality from which they emerge.

This relationship between the document and the open, exploratory form of poetic writing was crucial to Rukeyser's developing definition of poetic meaning. For her, poetry was not about indexing "facts"—but neither was it about creating "fictions." It was not about being good or beautiful: "for its desire [is] the beautiful, its desire [is] the good," she wrote in *The Life of Poetry*. In moving toward truth, poetry willingly risks error and dissolves customary distinctions between fact and fiction, appearance and reality. It invites us to live in "full" or "total response" to the world around us—an invitation that, paradoxically, allows us to performatively suspend the framework of human perspective that, by its very nature, precludes a "total" point of view.

An invitation, however, does not necessarily guarantee arrival. Crucial to understanding Rukeyser's sense of "totality"—and, from there, her conception of poetry more generally—is that poetry is, first and foremost, a *call*. The poem is not conceived *as* a "total response," that is, but as an invitation to give that kind of response—"to the earth, to each other, and to ourselves." The poem "requires"; it is, for Rukeyser, the very *act* of requiring. It is an evocation of totality, and of the contingent relationship between subject and object, self and other, which may never actually be consummated with a reply.

But even to evoke the possibility of a relationship with what exists beyond the bounds of subjective perspective and understanding is to take on a large, perhaps even an impossible, responsibility. It is the weight of this impossible responsibility that, Rukeyser suggests, we seem to crave "above all things." Describing her experience in the early days of the Spanish Civil War, she recalls that what she and the other foreign journalists wanted most was to bear witness to—and communicate the reality of—something beyond them, something they didn't understand. They wanted some voice—"deep, prophetic, direct"—to charge them with the supreme task of poetry; to say, "go home: tell your peoples what you have seen."

The supreme task of poetry, Rukeyser implies here, is the revelation of a larger and more complex reality than can ordinarily be seen. It consists of expressing that larger reality—but without denying or forgetting the subjective framework of this expression, or the material conditions that constitute it. By looking at the world not as it may appear *to* or *for* us, but instead at our processes of perception and at "relationships themselves," poetry both renders visible and disrupts borders. It addresses the limits of subjects, objects, and linear time in order to move past them, toward an "imaginative truth" more inclusive than (and yet certainly inclusive *of*) accepted scientific and historic truths.

"Art," Rukeyser reminds us, "is not in the world to deny any reality":

> You stand in the cave, the walls are on every side. The walls are real. But in the space between you and the walls, the images of everything you know, full of fire and possibility, life appearing as personal grace…There is here a reciprocal reality. It is the clue to art; and it needs its poetry.

Elaborating her own allegory of the cave, Rukeyser asks us to recognize the reality of our subjective frameworks (i.e., the walls that surround us), as well the "reciprocal reality" of our complicity in maintaining those frames, and our ability to reimagine them.

When *The Life of Poetry* was published in 1949, World War II had been over for just four years; the Soviet Union detonated its first atomic bomb, marking the beginning of the Cold War; in South Africa, apartheid became official government policy. "In a time of crisis," Rukeyser begins her book, "we summon our strength." In our own time of crisis, it seems especially pertinent that we summon the life of poetry: that we respond to Rukeyser's call to live in total response to the world around us, and endeavour to become "more human" by recognizing ourselves as *part* of—rather than the sole producers of—the reality of that world. It seems especially pertinent that we ask: How can we acknowledge the limits of language and selfhood and, at the same time, attempt to communicate past them? How can we make ourselves available to every possible reply?

Notes

"THE NOTHING THAT IS": AN ETHICS

1   Stevens resists personifying "nothing" in the manner of, for example, a poem like John Wilmot's philosophical and social satire "Upon Nothing," which casts "Nothing" in the role of a monarch and explains the relation between nothing and something in genealogical terms:

> Ere time and place were, time and place were not,
> When primitive Nothing Something straight begot,
> Then all proceeded from the great united—What?

2   "I repeat that his role is to help people to live their lives. He has had immensely to do with giving life whatever savor it possesses. He has had to do with whatever the imagination and the senses have made of the world."

3   Fred Moten refers to "difference without separability" in a talk titled "Performance and Blackness" that he delivered at the Museum of Modern Art in Warsaw, Poland, in June 2014. He goes on to invite his mostly white audience "to claim rather than to disavow this condition that is already ours...which is entanglement, vulnerability, the non-full, being both more than and less than ourselves."

4   This follows quite naturally, of course, if we are to acknowledge the post-structuralist thinking of Foucault or Derrida. Both of these thinkers explore the way myth and literature are foundational to scientific discourse—thus emphasizing that a distinction between poetic and scientific discourses has never been clear.

5   According to Heidegger's definition of the term, *poiesis* denotes the arrival or "presencing" of that which "is not yet" into what is—a definition he draws from a sentence in Plato's *Symposium*, which reads: "Every occasion for whatever passes over and goes forward into presencing from that which is not presencing is *poiēsis*, is bringing forth."

6   In Stevens's "The Man with the Blue Guitar," he writes of "a tune beyond us, yet ourselves, A tune...Of things exactly as they are." When the guitarist strums, he sounds "sudden rightnesses" and achieves the "finding of a satisfaction." "What might rightness mean here?" asks Critchley.

"At its best, modern poetry achieves the experience of a sudden rightness that can be crystallized in a word, a name or a sound, the twanging of a blue guitar...Poetry intensifies experience by suddenly suspending it, withdrawing one from it, and lighting up not some otherworldly obscurities, but what Emerson in 'The American Scholar' calls 'the near, the low, the common.'"

7   Stevens's suggestion in "The Emperor of Ice Cream," for example, to "let be be finale of seem," in no way absolves the distinctly "aspectual" stance of the poem itself that builds and arrives at its meaning according to suggestion and association rather than through the assignation of fixed identities and values.

8   "One day we may not distinguish (other than for knowledge) what creates from what is created, living man from the living universe," speculates Édouard Glissant in *Poetic Intention*:

> The poem reaches toward that indistinction which is not confusion but synthesis (it announces it absolutely and renders it each time possible); and the synthesis in turn is neither interlace nor mechanism, but projection and maturation forever postponed. Thus the poem consumes itself in that future.

9   Anaximander's "aperion" describes the "limitless" or "inexpressible" essence of all things. "The aperion is understood to be a similar concept to Chaos," explains Tyler, "the original state of the 'gaping void' or vacuum that nevertheless incorporates energy from which the universe originates. Since he never clearly defines the term, however, saying that the essence of all things is the aperion amounts to a tautology, that the essence of all things is the universal essence. This leaves us with the conceptual void that we are staring into an answer that has no meaning." It is this tautological structure that Stevens's poem specifically avoids.

BARBARIANS AMONG US

1   "To write poetry after Auschwitz is barbaric," wrote Adorno in his 1951 essay "Cultural Criticism and Society": "And this corrodes even the knowledge of why it has become impossible to write poetry today. Absolute reification, which presupposed intellectual progress as one of its elements, is now preparing to absorb the mind entirely. Critical intelligence cannot be equal to this challenge as long as it confines itself to self-satisfied contemplation."

2   "Celan's negative poetics give voice," writes Daniel Feldman in his essay "Writing Nothing," "to the survivor's vertiginous experience of the impossible becoming possible, of non-being mingling with being, of nothing in fact existing." His poetry also charges readers with a "moral calling": "If the result of extreme historic trauma such as the Shoah is to destroy the individual subject, then it is the work of genocide literature to 'I,' to '*ichten*.' The reader's responsibility is to oppose *vernichten* [annihilation] and to engage in a process of *ichten* [I-ing; as in Celan's poem "Once": "One and Infinite/ annihilated/I-ing"] whereby we restore subjectivity to the victims. To do so one must learn to read between lines, letters and sounds in order to hear silent and concealed words."

"IF I WERE HUMAN"

1   As Agamben observes, "To define the human not through any *nota characteristica*, but rather through his self-knowledge, means that man is the being which recognizes itself as such, that *man is the animal that must recognize itself as human to be human*."

"REFLOATING" THE FALLING MAN

1 The "falling man" photograph—part of a series taken by photographer Richard Drew just moments after the Twin Towers attack of September 11, 2001—was published widely in the days following the attack, but then retracted. As *Time Magazine* puts it in their commentary on the one hundred "most influential photos of all time," the photograph, which pictures "one man's distinct escape from the collapsing buildings," was seen as "a symbol of individuality against the backdrop of faceless skyscrapers. On a day of mass tragedy, Falling Man is one of the only widely seen pictures that shows someone dying." Because of this, the commentary continues, "it can be a difficult image to process, the man perfectly bisecting the iconic towers like an arrow" (100photos .time.com/photos/richard-drew-falling-man).

2 In his "Theses on the Philosophy of History," Walter Benjamin famously wrote: "The tradition of the oppressed teaches us that the 'state of emergency' in which we live is not the exception but the rule. We must attain to a conception of history that is in keeping with this insight. Then we shall clearly realize that it is our task to bring about a real state of emergency, and this will improve our position in the struggle against Fascism. One reason why Fascism has a chance is that in the name of progress its opponents treat it as a historical norm. The current amazement that the things we are experiencing are 'still' possible in the twentieth century is *not* philosophical. This amazement is not the beginning of knowledge—unless it is the knowledge that the view of history which gives rise to it is untenable."

ABSENCE IN "THE SYSTEM"

1 "It is high time," writes Marx, "that Communists should openly, in the face of the whole world, publish their views, their aims, their tendencies, and meet this nursery tale of the Spectre of Communism with a manifesto of the party itself."

POETIC EMERGENCY

1 In poetry that is "authentic and great," Heidegger once wrote, "an essential superiority reigns over everything which is purely science" (quoted in Alain Badiou's *Infinite Thought*).

"IF WE DARE TO"

1 "Here I wanted people to go forth out of my book and read," Moure commented upon reading an earlier draft of this essay. "I wanted them to actively break the border of my book, its (im) possible hegemony, to go read outside it, to go on reading..

2 "A minor literature doesn't come from a minor language; it is rather that which a minority constructs within a major language," write Deleuze and Guattari in *Kafka*. "But the first characteristic of minor literature in any case is that in it language is affected with a high coefficient of deterritorialization."

VISUAL HISTORIES

1 Gustav Metzger founded the auto-destructive art movement in the late 1950s. He articulated its aims in his 1959 manifesto, "Auto-Destructive Art" (quoted in Kristine Stiles's *Theories and Documents of Contemporary Art: A Sourcebook of Artists' Writings*):

Auto-destructive art is primarily a form of public art for industrial societies.

Self-destructive painting, sculpture and construction is a total unity of idea, site, form, colour, method, and timing of the disintegrative process.

Auto-destructive art can be created with natural forces, traditional art techniques and technological techniques.

The amplified sound of the auto-destructive process can be an element of the total conception.

The artist may collaborate with scientists, engineers.

Self-destructive art can be machine produced and factory assembled.

2   From W. H. Auden's "In Memory of W. B. Yeats": "For poetry makes nothing happen: it survives / In the valley of its making where executives / Would never want to tamper, flows on south / From ranches of isolation and the busy griefs, / Raw towns that we believe and die in; it survives, / A way of happening, a mouth."

3   In Alberto Toscano and Jeff Kinkle's recent exploration of the limits of representation, *Cartographies of the Absolute*, they explain that the title of their project was chosen "because of how it encapsulates the problem of visualizing or narrating capitalism today. As the science or craft of map-making, cartography connotes a technical endeavour, judged by its accuracy…The 'absolute' is a theological and then a philosophical category, gesturing towards that which defies representation, which, contrasted to our mortal perception, is infinite and unencompassed." The effects of capitalism are hard to see precisely because we measure those effects according to the linear narratives of progress that also structure our own subject positions. What Toscano and Kinkle suggest, in effect, is a *poetics* of capitalism in which the invisible forces of capital and capitalist structures are made palpable through the subject's confrontation with the limits of subjectivity, and of representation itself.

4   A chronology of Gustav Metzger's life includes the following concise entry, dated "Summer, 1944": "Decides to become a sculptor instead of a professional revolutionary." The next entry, "August, 1944," reports that Metzger "gets a job at Chamneys nature-cure clinic near Tring as a gardener" and "begins to carve small pieces of stone."

Best known as the founder of the auto-destructive art movement, Metzger has long sought to integrate political activism and art through an exploration of the limits of—and potential interstices between—subjective and collective experience, aesthetic questioning and political statement, abstract concept and material form. Within the void space of *Null Object*, what we glimpse is a visual representation of these intersections and a material enactment of Metzger's decision from August 1944 to become an artist rather than a revolutionary: Metzger's effort to think past the boundaries imposed by positive ideas and forms (i.e., to think of nothing) is presented within and as a material index of history and time.

A "MOST HUMAN" CALL

1   For further discussion of the concept of the human and what it might mean to "be more human" see the earlier essay, "If I were human": Reflections on One Hundred Years of War."

Works Cited

Adorno, Theodor. *Prisms: Essays in Cultural Criticism and Society*. Ed. Shierry Weber Nicholsen and Samuel Weber. Cambridge, MA: MIT Press, 1983.
———. *Negative Dialectics*. Trans. E. B. Ashton. New York and London: Continuum Press, 1973.
Agamben, Giorgio. *The End of the Poem: Studies in Poetics*. Trans. Daniel Heller-Roazen. Stanford, CA: Stanford UP, 1996.
———. *Homo Sacer: Sovereign Power and Bare Life*. Trans. Daniel Heller-Roazen. Stanford: Stanford UP, 1998.
———. *Language and Death*. Trans. Karen E. Pinkus and Michael Hardt. Minneapolis and London: U of Minnesota P, 2006.
———. *The Open: Man and Animal*. Trans. Kevin Attell. Stanford: Stanford UP, 2004.
———. *State of Exception*. Trans. Kevin Attell. Chicago: U of Chicago P, 2005.
Altieri, Charles. *Wallace Stevens and the Demands of Modernity: Toward Phenomenology of Value*. Ithaca, NY: Cornell UP, 2013.
Aristotle. *Poetics*. Trans. Stephen Halliwell. Cambridge and London: Harvard UP, 1995.
Ashbery, John. *Selected Poems*. New York, NY: Penguin Books, 1986.
Auden, W. H. *Collected Poems*. New York, NY: Vintage, 1991.
Badiou, Alain. *Infinite Thought*. Trans. Oliver Feltham and Justin Clemens. London: Continuum Press, 2011.
Baker, Gerard. "Trump, 'Lies,' and Honest Journalism." *Wall Street Journal*. January 4, 2017. www.wsj.com/articles/trump-lies-and-honest-journalism-1483557700. Accessed May 7, 2019.
Benjamin, Walter. *Selected Writings*, Vol. 2, part 2. Ed. Michael Jennings et al. Cambridge, MA and London, UK: Belknap Press of Harvard UP, 1999.
Benjamin, Walter. *Illuminations*. Ed. Hannah Arendt. Trans. Harry Zohn. New York, NY: Schocken Books, 1969.
Boletsi, Maria. *Barbarism and its Discontents*. Stanford, CA: Stanford UP, 2013.
Breytenbach, Breyten. "Mandela's Smile: Notes on South Africa's Failed Revolution." *Harper's Magazine*. December 2008.
Carson, Anne. *Decreation: Poetry, Essays, Opera*. New York, NY: Knopf, 2005.
Celan, Paul. *Poems of Paul Celan: A Bilingual German/English Edition*. Trans. Michael Hamburger. New York, NY: Persea Press, 2002.
Cixous, Hélène. *Three Steps on the Ladder of Writing*. Trans. Susan Sellers and Sarah Cornell. New York, NY: Columbia UP, 1994.

Critchley, Simon. *Things Merely Are: Philosophy in the Poetry of Wallace Stevens.* New York, NY: Routledge, 2005.

Culler, Jonathan. *Theory of the Lyric.* Cambridge and London: Harvard UP, 2015.

Deleuze, Gilles, and Félix Guattari. *Kafka: Toward a Minor Literature.* Trans. Dana Polan. Minneapolis and London: U of Minnesota P, 1986.

Della Volpe, Galvano. *Critique of Taste.* Trans. Michael Caesar. New York, NY: Schocken Books, 1978.

Derrida, Jacques. *On Touching.* Trans. Christine Irizarry. Stanford: Stanford UP, 2005.

———. *Specters of Marx.* Trans. Peggy Kamuf. New York, NY: Routledge, 2006.

———. *Writing and Difference.* Trans. Alan Bass. London and New York: Routledge, 1978.

Duras, Marguerite. *Writing.* Trans. Mark Polizzotti. Minneapolis, MN, and London, UK: U of Minnesota P, 2011.

Emerson, Ralph Waldo. *Ralph Waldo Emerson.* Ed. Richard Poirier. Oxford: Oxford UP, 1990.

Eskin, Michael. *Ethics and Dialogue: In the Works of Levinas, Bakhtin, Mandel'shtam, and Celan.* Oxford: Oxford UP, 2000.

Fanon, Franz. *The Wretched of the Earth.* Trans. Richard Philcox. New York, NY: Grove Press, 2004.

Feldman, Dan. "Writing nothing: Negation and Subjectivity in the Holocaust Poetry of Paul Celan and Dan Pagis." *Comparative Literature,* 2014.

Ferran, Bronac. "Sculpting the Void: Between Negation and Abnegation, Between Action and Absence." *Null Object.* Ed. Bruce Gilchrist and Jo Joelson, pp. 30–47. London: Black Dog Publishing, 2013.

Gerwarth, Robert. *The Vanquished: Why the First World War Failed to End.* New York, NY: Farrar, Strauss and Giroux, 2016.

Gardner, Thomas. *Regions of Unlikeness: Explaining Contemporary Poetry.* Lincoln and London: University of Nebraska, 1999.

Gilchrist, Bruce and Jo Joelson. *Null Object.* London: Black Dog Publishing, 2013.

Glissant, Édouard. *Poetic Intention.* Trans. Nathalie Stephens. Callicoon, NY: Nightboat Books, 2010.

Gray, John. *The Immortalization Commission: Science and the Strange Quest to Cheat Death.* New York, NY: Farrar, Strauss and Giroux, 2011.

Heidegger, Martin. *The Question Concerning Technology, and Other Essays.* Trans. William Lovitt. New York, NY: Harper Collins, 1982.

Hejinian, Lyn. *The Language of Inquiry.* Berkeley, CA: U of California P, 2000.

Irigaray, Luce. *Sharing the World.* New York, NY: Continuum Press, 2008.

James, William. *Principles of Psychology, Vol. 1.* New York, NY: H. Holt, 1918.

Kulik, Gary. *War Stories: False Atrocity Tales, Swift Boaters, and Winter Soldiers—What Really Happened in Vietnam.* Lincoln, NE: Potomac Books, 2009.

Marsh, James, Simon Chinn, and Phillippe Petit. *Man on Wire.* Film. Magnolia Pictures, 2008.

Marx, Karl. *The Communist Manifesto.* Trans. Samuel Moore. New York, NY: Pocket Books, 1964.

Marx, Karl. *Writings of the Young Marx on Philosophy and Society.* Trans. Lloyd David Easton and Kurt H. Guddat. Garden City, NY: Doubleday, 1967.

Mason, Jeffrey D. *Stone Tower: The Political Theater of Arthur Miller.* Ann Arbor: U of Michigan P, 2008.

McCann, Colum. *Let the Great World Sing.* New York: Harper Collins, 2009.

Metzger, Gustav. *Damaged Nature, Auto Destructive Art.* London, UK: Coracle Press, 1996.

Hardesty, Kendra. Interview in "Military to Investigate Video of Apparent Desecration," *Wall Street Journal.* January 12, 2012. www.wsj.com/articles/SB10001424052970204124204577155331507066696. Accessed May 7, 2019.

Miller, Arthur. "All My Sons." *Collected Plays 1944–1961.* New York: The Library of America. 2006.

Morris, Errol. *Believing is Seeing: Observations on the Mysteries of Photography.* New York, NY: Penguin Books, 2014.

———. "Will the Real Hooded Man Please Stand Up." *New York Times.* August 15, 2017. opinionator.blogs.nytimes.com/2007/08/15/will-the-real-hooded-man-please-stand-up/. Accessed May 7, 2019.

Moure, Erín. *My Beloved Wager*. Edmonton: NeWest Press, 2009.

Nancy, Jean-Luc. *The Sense of the World*. Trans. Jeffrey S. Librett. Minneapolis: U of Minnesota P, 1997.

———. *O Cidadán*. Toronto: House of Anansi Press, 2002.

Nicholls, Peter. *George Oppen and the Fate of Modernism*. Oxford and New York: Oxford UP, 2007.

Nyamuya Maogoto, Jackson. *Reading the Shadows of History: The Turkish and Ethiopian 'Internationalized' Domestic Crime Trials*. Ed. Kevin Heller and Gerry Simpson. Oxford, UK: Oxford UP, 2013.

Oppen, George. *New Collected Poems*. Ed. Michael Davidson. New York: New Directions, 2008.

———. *The Selected Letters of George Oppen*. Ed. Rachel Blau DuPlessis. Durham and London: Duke UP, 1990.

Otten, Terry. *The Temptation of Innocence in the Dramas of Arthur Miller*. Columbia and London: U of Missouri P, 2002.

The Oxford English Dictionary. Online edition. March 2016. Oxford University Press. www.oed.com .ezproxy.library.arizona.edu/view/Entry/221704?redirectedFrom=vatic&. Accessed May 25, 2016.

Paterson, Katie. katiepaterson.org. Accessed May 7, 2019.

Philip, M. Nourbese. *Zong!* Toronto, ON: Mercury Press, 2008.

Poirier, Richard. *Poetry and Pragmatism*. Cambridge, Mass.: Harvard UP, 1992.

Pratt, Mary Louise. "Arts of the Contact Zone." In *Literatures in Contiguity: Québecois Canadian Cultural Spaces*, ed. Catherine LeClerc et al. Montreal: Concordia University Bookstore, 2008.

Rudy, Susan. "'what can atmospheres with/vocabularies delight?': Excessively Reading Erín Moure." In *Writing in Our Time: Canada's Radical Poetries in English (1957–2003)*, ed. Pauline Butling and Susan Rudy. Waterloo, ON: Wilfrid Laurier UP, 2005.

Rukeyser, Muriel. *The Life of Poetry*. Middletown, CT: Wesleyan UP, 1996.

Sampson, Fiona. "Symphony of Sighs" (review of Carson's *Decreation*). *Guardian*, September 23, 2006. www.theguardian.com/books/2006/sep/23/featuresreviews.guardianreview29. Accessed May 7, 2019.

Scott, A. O. "Walking on Air Between Towers" *New York Times*, July 25, 2008.

Shelley, Mary. *Frankenstein*. Hertfordshire, UK: Wordsworth Editions, 1993.

Singer, Henry. *The Falling Man*. Film. Channel 4, 2006.

Singer, Peter. *Wired for War: The Robotics Revolution and Conflict in the 21st Century*. New York, NY: Penguin Books, 2009.

Stevens, Wallace. *Collected Poetry and Prose*. Ed. Frank Kermode and Joan Richardson. New York, NY: Literary Classics of the United States, Inc., 1997.

Stiles, Kristine, Ed. *Theories and Documents of Contemporary Art: A Sourcebook of Artists' Writings*. 2nd Ed. Berkeley, Los Angeles and London: U of California P, 2012.

Taylor, Charles. "Calling a Lie a Lie." *Boston Globe*. January 24, 2017. www.bostonglobe.com/opinion/2017/01/24/calling-lie-lie/yclDCEnPvG4y7BvUNJrmdO/story.html. Accessed May 7, 2019.

Toscano, Alberto and Jeff Kinkle. *Cartographies of the Absolute*. Alresford, UK: Zero Books, 2015.

Tyler, Christopher. "Null Object: Proegomena." *Null Object*. Ed. Bruce Gilchrist and Jo Joelson, pp. 30–47. London: Black Dog Publishing, 2013.

Venable Moore, Catherine, "The Book of the Dead." *Best American Essays 2017*. Ed. Leslie Jamison. Boston and NY: Houghton Mifflin, 2017.

Weil, Simone. *Gravity and Grace*. New York and London: Verso, 2003.

Wilmot, John. *Collected Works of John Wilmot Earl of Rochester*. London, UK: Nonesuch Press, 1926.

Woolf, Virginia. *A Writer's Diary: Being Extracts from the Diary of Virginia Woolf*. Ed. Leonard Woolf. San Diego, New York and London: Harcourt, Inc., 1954.

———. *The Waves*. Oxford, UK: Oxford UP, 2015.

Wynter, Sylvia. "Unsettling the Coloniality of Being/Power/Truth/Freedom: Towards the Human, After Man, Its Overrepresentation—An Argument." *CR: New Centennial Review* 3.3 (2003).

Acknowledgements

With thanks to the many people who either helped to inspire, or who read and commented on these essays at various stages: Amaryll Chanady, Sol Davis, Liz Johnston, John Melillo, Andrew John Miller, Erín Moure, Lianne Moyes, Tenney Nathanson, Taiwo Adetunji Osinubi, Eric Savoy, Robert Schwartzwald, Rebecca Silver Slayter, Janet Shively, Joshua Marie Wilkinson.

Special thanks to Julie Joosten for her enthusiasm, encouragement, and editorial suggestions, which helped this project take shape. And to Rachael Wilson for the care and thoughtfulness with which she helped, and challenged me, to bring the project to completion. Thank you also to Jay and Hazel MillAr, Stuart Ross, and everyone at Book*hug for their generosity and support.

Versions of several of these essays have appeared, sometimes in a radically different form, in the following publications: *Texte, Image et Sons* (Université de Paris à Créteil, Spring 2019); *Brick* (Toronto, Issue 99, Summer 2017); *Anne Carson: Ecstatic Lyre*. Ed. Joshua Marie Wilkinson (University of Michigan Press, February 2015); *Evening Will Come: A Monthly Journal of Poetics. The VOLTA* (Issue 36, December 2013); *Antithesis* (University of Melbourne, Vol. 20: FEAR issue,

Spring 2010); *Cosmonauts Avenue* (Montreal, December 2014); *The Brock Review* (Brock University, Vol. 11, No. 1, July 2010).

The image *Null Object* is reprinted with kind permission of London Fieldworks.

PHOTO: CHRISTINE WHELAN-HACHEY

JOHANNA SKIBSRUD is a novelist, poet and Assistant Professor of English at the University of Arizona. Her debut novel, *The Sentimentalists*, was awarded the 2010 Scotiabank Giller Prize, making her the youngest writer to win Canada's most prestigious literary prize. The book was subsequently shortlisted for the Commonwealth Book Award and is currently translated into five languages. *The New York Times Book Review* describes her second novel, *Quartet for the End of Time* (2014), as a "haunting" exploration of "the complexity of human relationships and the myriad ways in which identity can be malleable." Johanna is also the author of a third novel, *Island* (Hamish Hamilton Canada 2019), two collections of short fiction, a children's book, and three books of poetry. Her latest poetry collection, *The Description of the World* (2016), was the recipient of the 2017 Canadian Author's Association for Poetry and the 2017 Fred Cogswell Award. A critical monograph titled *The Poetic Imperative: A Speculative Aesthetics* is forthcoming from McGill-Queen's University Press in spring 2020.

ESSAIS SERIES

Drawing on the Old and Middle French definitions of *essai*, meaning first "trial" and then "attempt," and from which the English word "essay" emerges, the works in the Essais Series challenge traditional forms and styles of cultural enquiry. The Essais Series is committed to publishing works concerned with justice, equity, and diversity. It supports texts that draw on seemingly intractable questions, to ask them anew and to elaborate these questions. The books in the Essais Series are forms of vital generosity; they invite attention to a necessary reconsideration of culture, society, politics and experience.

TITLES IN THE ESSAIS SERIES:

Her Paraphernalia: On Motherlines, Sex, Blood, Loss & Selfies
by Margaret Christakos (2016)

Notes from a Feminist Killjoy: Essays on Everyday Life
by Erin Wunker (2016)

Blank: Essays and Interviews
by M. NourbeSe Philip (2017)

My Conversations with Canadians
by Lee Maracle (2017)

Dear Current Occupant
by Chelene Knight (2018)

Refuse: CanLit in Ruins
co-edited by Hannah McGregor, Julie Rak, and Erin Wunker (2018)

Before I Was a Critic I Was a Human Being
by Amy Fung (2019)

Disquieting: Essays on Silence
by Cynthia Cruz (2019)

The Nothing that Is: Essays on Art, Literature and Being
by Johanna Skibsrub (2019)

On Beauty, or Where Things Touch
by Bahar Orang (2020)

For more information and to order visit bookhugpress.ca

Manufactured as the first edition of
The Nothing That Is: Essays on Art, Literature and Being
in the fall of 2019 by Book*hug Press

Edited for the press by Rachael Guynn Wilson
Copy edited by Stuart Ross
Type + design by Ingrid Paulson

bookhugpress.ca